Caught in the Act

Also by Toinette Lippe

Nothing Left Over: A Plain and Simple Life

Caught in the Act

Reflections on Being, Knowing, and Doing

Toinette Lippe

JEREMY P. TARCHER · PENGUIN

a member of Penguin Group (USA) Inc.

New York

Most Tarcher/Penguin books are available at special quantity discounts for bulk purchase for sales promotions, premiums, fundraising, and educational needs. Special books or book excerpts also can be created to fit specific needs. For details, write Penguin Group (USA) Inc. Special Markets, 375 Hudson Street, New York, NY 10014.

Jeremy P. Tarcher/Penguin
a member of
Penguin Group (USA) Inc.
375 Hudson Street
New York, NY 10014
www.penguin.com

Library of Congress Cataloging-in-Publication Data

Lippe, Toinette, date.
Caught in the act : reflections on being, knowing, and doing / Toinette Lippe.
p.   cm.
ISBN 1-58542-346-7
1. Conduct of life. I. Title.
BJ1581.2.L53   2004   2004047886
170'.44—dc22

Printed in the United States of America
1   3   5   7   9   10   8   6   4   2

This book is printed on acid-free paper. ∞

Book design by Meighan Cavanaugh

JM

A deep bow to my three warmhearted and
wonderful e-muses, Sara Jenkins, Margaret Dodd,
and Marcia Fields, who encouraged me at every
turn along the path of self-discovery

Contents

When my son Adam learned that I was writing another book, he said, "How can you write a sequel to something called *Nothing Left Over?*" So perhaps a word of explanation is in order. My first book focused on simplifying and paring down. This one is about opening up and exploring. Different threads weave in and out of the tapestry of my life, appearing, disappearing, and then surfacing again. And, as last time, the details are personal, but the perceptions and whatever insights you may find here are common to us all.

T.L.

Caught in the Act

Human Being

To see, purely and simply, without name,
Without expectations, fears, or hopes,
At the edge where there is no I or not-I.

"THIS ONLY," CZESLAW MILOSZ, *translated by Robert Hass*

 A three-day weekend and nothing to do. I had been working hard for months, and now that everything appeared to have been taken care of, I felt becalmed. I cast about in my mind for an appropriate something to fill the empty time.

Someone had sent me an interesting-looking book, *Going Native,* by Tom Harmer, about an Anglo seeking Native American wisdom from a Salish elder in the Pacific Northwest. The evening it arrived I opened it and began to read. Not only was it exquisitely written—reminiscent of Cormac McCarthy's novel *All the Pretty Horses*—but it was extraordinarily powerful. And, as usual, it offered me precisely what I needed to hear in that moment:

> "That how the crazy White man take back his sickness," Clayton said, shaking his head. "To be the natural man, same as all the world around, that not good enough. Gotta get busy. Gotta worry and lose touch with what's real so he feel okay inside. The White man not feel good enough, not worthy just to be alive in this world. Have to prove something. Race against each other to be something more. But what? If a man is alive, here in this world, he have that right to be here, that's all. Not anything we have to do to deserve this life, be worthy of it. Just accept it, live it, remember it."

Tom Harmer goes into the wilderness, exploring forests and rivers, to find himself, to understand what a human being is. But surely it is possible to learn the same lesson here in this busy metropolis where our lives are almost defined by stress? It is just as important to comprehend this truth here in Manhattan, to live it, and by coming into contact with so many people, to share the knowledge by embodying it in our lives each day.

Now that I think back, I realize that this idea is not new to me. Two memories surface. Almost thirty years ago I was at the zoo with a photographer from East Germany. We were standing in front of a cage gazing at two brilliantly colored toucans sitting side-by-side on a branch, and he asked me, "What do birds do all day?" Without a moment's hesitation, I replied, "Birds don't do; birds just are."

On another occasion I complained to someone that I didn't know how I would occupy myself during a transatlantic flight to London. He looked at me strangely and pointed out that it wasn't necessary for me to do anything. That was the crew's job. All I had to do was sit there.

It is sad that it has taken me so long to attempt to put this into practice. And it is ironic that I was moved to put these thoughts down on paper because I had reached that blessed state of nondoing. True to form, I immediately began to fill the vacuum with more doing. I sat down and started typing. But at least this time I have noticed it.

Not only do we spend most of our lives "doing" something, we tend to believe that we are what we do. In the United States, when people are introduced, their first question is "What do you do?" and my usual response is "I am an editor (or a writer)" rather than "I edit (or write)." Yet the inquiry was not about who I was but what I did. So many of us get "caught in the act."

Back in 1837 Ralph Waldo Emerson addressed the Phi Beta Kappa Society at Harvard in a speech known as "The American Scholar." In it he described how we have somehow forgotten who we are:

> The planter, who is Man sent out into the field to gather food, is seldom cheered by any idea of the true dignity of his ministry. He sees his bushel and his cart, and nothing beyond, and sinks into the farmer, instead of Man on the farm. The tradesman scarcely ever gives an ideal worth to his work, but is ridden by the routine of his craft, and the soul is subject to dollars. The priest becomes a form; the attorney, a statute-book; the mechanic, a machine; the sailor, a rope of a ship. In this distribution of functions, the scholar is the delegated intellect. In the right state, he is, *Man Thinking.* In the degenerate state, when the victim of society, he tends to become a mere thinker, or, still worse, the parrot of other men's thinking.

When I say that I am an editor, what I am saying is that my main identity is what I do to pay the rent and put food on the table, whether I enjoy doing that or not. Wouldn't it be nice if I felt free enough to respond, "I paint, I garden, and I enjoy listening to music. During the work week I also edit books and

4

write"? Yet that is not the way we tend to see ourselves, and so it is not how we answer. Also, of course, when people ask us what we do, they are seeking to pigeonhole us, to get a handle on how they should view us, and to find out whether, perhaps, they are in the same industry and might have friends or colleagues in common. The inquiry about what someone does is a way to discover a great deal about a new acquaintance, but it is also very restrictive and limiting, particularly if the answer is one word, like "editor." My response implies that this is not just what I do but who I am, that I have completely identified with whatever function I fulfill during the work week. I am not saying that it is wrong to tell people how you earn your living. I am pointing out that this is only one aspect of you and there are a host of others that are equally important. It is a well-known fact that when people lose their jobs or retire, they often find themselves in a kind of limbo because that identification has been severed, and they have to find their feet again and explore other parts of their being.

This is a heavy burden we all carry around, and it obscures so much from our view. We see neither our own lives clearly nor the lives of any of the people we meet for the first time. When I go home to England, where people hardly ever discuss their work, no one asks me anything about what I do, and I get the sense that a large part of my life has been amputated. I am so used to talking about what I do that when that opportunity is removed, I feel bereft.

Another aspect of all this is that as long as I think of myself as an editor, I am frozen in that role. It doesn't occur to me that perhaps I could use those same skills, or others I might have, to do different work. We identify with a particular role and thus become typecast, like an actress who plays an ingénue in her first and second appearances, and her third, and then finds it hard even to get considered for a different role. So we are never stretched. In the job that I held at Knopf for thirty-two years selling paperback rights, I had begun to feel like a piece of old furniture. No one even noticed that I was still there because I and my role had become so familiar to them that they no longer questioned it or me.

Some years ago I met a small boy who asked me "What are you?" and I was completely floored. Perhaps he was asking what I did for a living and phrasing it in a much more appropriate way for the answer "I'm an editor," or maybe he wanted to know my name, but it shook me out of my complacency while I considered his question on an existential level. A line from Psalm 8 flashed into my mind: "What is man that thou art mindful of him?" My world opened up as I realized how much more I was (or could be) than what I do, either for a living or in any given moment.

The most frequent question passersby put to me when I am working in the community garden in Riverside Park is "What is the name of that flower?" People believe that if they know the name of something, they know what it really is. I see this happening in my own life also—but the whole thing is an illusion. Knowing the name assigned to something does not bring us any closer to realizing its essence. In many ways it prevents true understanding because by naming something, we come to believe that the description *is* the thing itself. We put labels on objects and people and then see only the labels. We never actually see who or what is in front of us. Labels are a form of limitation: "This is (or I am) just this much and no more." I may be an editor or a writer, but I'm also an Englishwoman, a mother, a sister, a friend, an almost-Buddhist, an inveterate traveler, an ardent linguist, a beginning gardener, a painter of flowers, a yoga and tai chi practitioner, an avid dictionary and atlas reader, and so on. And even if you added up all these attributes or ways of categorizing me, that wouldn't tell you who I am. Yet we all assume that articulating our views of how other people appear to us gives us insight into their nature. We don't want to acknowledge that people are processes, not fixed identities. We are masterpieces in the making, and at any minute everything could shift.

Years ago I attended a conference on "inner science" at Amherst College, where the Dalai Lama was the main speaker. On my arrival a young woman asked me "Are you a Buddhist?" I said "No," because to me a Buddhist is someone who has taken refuge in the Buddha, the Sangha, and the Dharma and made a commitment to a sangha as well, and I have done none of those things. Her next question was "So what are you then?" This seemed an invasive and rather rude question, and after a moment's hesitation, I replied, "I am a person."

In her book *Reflections on a Mountain Lake*, the Tibetan Buddhist nun Ani Tenzin Palmo points out that most of the time we experience only ideas, interpretations, and comparisons and not things themselves. She also says that the boredom and meaninglessness so many people complain about stems from the quality of awareness with which we live our lives. In describing the instant rapport people sense when they are lucky enough to meet the Dalai Lama, she writes: "People are accustomed to being related to as a reporter or as a politician or whatever. But the Dalai Lama cuts through all that. He just relates from heart to heart."

In 2000, when my son Adam graduated from college and started work, I felt that I had paid my dues to society and, much to everyone's surprise, I quit my full-time job. I continued as editorial director of Bell Tower, the spiritual imprint I had founded in 1989, in a freelance capacity, and began to explore other things life had to offer. Until that moment work had been the most important thing in one way or another, and I wanted to discover how to play, something that had eluded me for far too long. It was a little late to begin to play at sixty-one, but I thought it worth a try. Unless I was willing to make a major shift I knew that I would just keep putting one foot in front of the other, working harder and harder, until my life was over.

I felt as though my whole life had consisted of effort—or perhaps I should say Effort. Making a fresh start was vital. Perhaps if I stopped trying to "get things right" and just watched to see what would happen. . . . The state of the planet, the fraught situation in the Middle East, my uncertain future in the workplace—everything had brought me to this point, and the most appropriate response was "Glory be."

I began to study oriental brushpainting a few years

ago, and friends are always encouraging me to think of my painting as play. "Just let yourself go," they chorus. "Don't think about the correct or incorrect way of doing it. Experiment. Have a good time. Enjoy yourself." Yes, I know this is good advice, but I find it hard to carry out. Why is advice so difficult to accept? In the back of my head is a little voice that comments all the time, comparing what is happening with what might be happening or should be happening. How to persuade this eternal taskmistress to take a vacation? If she could have some fun, maybe she would let me do the same. But at the moment it's nag, nag, nag, as she compares the brush strokes on the paper to some imaginary strokes in my mind. Ah, perhaps the solution lies in perfecting the strokes in my mind. I recall now that the Israeli bodyworker Moshe Feldenkrais recommended visualizing movements in the mind if it was not possible to do them physically. A ballet dancer who had her leg in a cast for months performed her steps in her head every day, and once she was back on her feet was able to pick up where she had left off.

Something happened recently that seems to bode well. On my way home from a painting class I started to see the trees in Central Park in terms of brush strokes. It was quite a revelation. It reminded me of the time I caught my Chinese brushpainting friend, Charles Chu, sketching a scene in the air with an imaginary brush in his hand. When I saw him doing this I thought he was crazy, but now I am not so sure.

I need to admit that until I stop treating everything I do as work rather than play, I'm unlikely to enjoy any of it. No wonder I experience such reluctance to sit down and write or paint. I have to almost force myself to do either of them. As I have told many people, I have not so far enjoyed the act of writing, but I definitely enjoy reading what I have written. I felt the same way when I used to play the piano first thing in the morning. I didn't enjoy the playing itself. I enjoyed it only when the music sounded good. And that was, in the end, why I stopped practicing, although the reason I gave everyone else was that I didn't have the time once I became a mother. Back then a friend asked me, "So if you are not enjoying it, why do it?" It took me some time to digest this because I had put so much time and effort into learning how to play. Yet she was right, and in the end, I simply gave it up and thus avoided the issue. Or so I thought. Now, of course, the question of enjoyment is very real once more, and it is begging to be answered.

Here I am in semi-retirement, the point of which

is to do the things I enjoy and not have to do the things I don't enjoy, and I am still driving myself to do the things I believe I ought to enjoy. I know in my heart that most things can be enjoyable if one just approaches them with the right attitude. And that attitude is one of play, not drudgery. No more metaphorical gritting of my teeth. I have nothing to lose, so why am I not willing to take the plunge? I am keeping myself in a prison when the whole world is out there for my delight. I have to discover how to release my right brain so that its activity is not continually subordinated to what my left brain tells it is the approved (and therefore "best") way of doing things.

I need to provide the space and opportunity for play but not go about it as though it were one more task on my plate. To enter into it in a spirit of inquiry and amazement, ready for anything. With work, I believe I know how it ought to turn out. With play, I have no idea—which is probably a very good thing. One area of my life where I don't know better than anyone else. So this is a real blessing. There will be no "as if for the first time." It will *always* be the first time because I don't know how to do it and maybe never will.

One of the hurdles I have to surmount is the belief that enjoyment comes naturally when you are with someone else, that it is company I need. There is no denying that companionship can be great, but you certainly don't need to have someone else around to appreciate what is going on. My attitude is ridiculous, particularly since I do most things on my own now that I am working at home and not sharing my living space with anyone. When I looked at this sharp division between work and play, I came to the conclusion that I didn't know the mechanism for enjoying things. It is not that I don't enjoy many things. Of course I do. But I have the sense that enjoyment is something that happens spontaneously. So when I turn to activities like writing or painting in the hope that I will enjoy them, the exercise is doomed to failure.

What can I do to remedy this silly situation? Not load down particular activities with the expectation of enjoyment. Something loaded down is less likely to fly. It's the age-old problem of not working for results.

Instead of monitoring each activity as though I were a schoolmarm, I can marvel at what creation can manage on its own without my help. Recently I attended a concert and I noticed that the conductor was a little cramped for space and was standing at the very edge of the podium. So I kept my eye on her to make sure she didn't have an accident, as I have often kept my beady eye on drivers to make sure that their vehicles (if I am traveling in them) stay on the road. I did this once in the Himalayas with our Sikh bus driver. What did I think I could achieve from my seat in the middle of the bus? I was so full of terror at the thought of dropping thousands of feet to my death that I lost sight of the wonder of the mountains around me, mountains that I would probably never see again. And, of course, I lived to tell the tale.

The desire to get things right is instilled into most of us very early on in life, and it colors almost everything that follows. Parents and teachers go to great lengths to make sure that we understand how important it is to do things the proper way. I certainly did the same thing myself when I was bringing up Adam, but now I am wondering whether this aim shouldn't have been tempered somewhat. "Getting it right" implies that there is only one acceptable way to do everything when, of course, this is not the case. Just consider all the different ways people hold a pencil. Some grips are more comfortable than others, but the way I was taught to do it is certainly not the only way that works. Also, the first time I was taught how to paint bamboo, I was told that you start at the bottom of the stalk and push up but, later on, I read a book that told me to do the opposite.

When I was a child, my father would try to engage

me in conversation so that I could get some practice in either German or French, both of which he spoke fluently, having learned his trade in Germany and Switzerland. He would ask me a question in French and I would almost always clam up, not wanting to say anything unless I could express it perfectly. Again and again he would point out that it is better to say something rather than nothing. If you say something, you may not get it quite right, but other people will probably understand you. If you say nothing at all, then you are bound to be wrong. Of course, he was still using the paradigm of right and wrong to get his point across, but I didn't spot that at the time.

If you have a fixed idea in your mind that only one way is right, then, ipso facto, all other methods are wrong. This offers no latitude and means that much of what we attempt is doomed to failure. In addition, every action is infused with fear—the fear of failure.

I was brought up by a Victorian nanny and attended an English boarding school for seven years. So much was drilled into me in terms of black and white, even though the world is painted in many shades of gray (not to mention glorious color). It is this strict adherence to the rules—a presumption of what is right and what is wrong—that has got me this far in my life. But now is the time to let it go.

I was talking with a friend about how trying to get it right is the main obstacle I encounter in my painting and discovered that she has been experiencing this in her singing lessons. Her fear of not singing the notes correctly constricts and hampers the sound as it emerges from her throat. If we were walking beside the river, once we had a sense of how the path twisted and turned and what we needed to watch out for, we would probably be willing to skip along without worrying about falling into the water. With singing and painting, what is the worst that could happen to us? These are not life-threatening activities. We wouldn't even fall into the water if we made a mistake.

So why are our fear and doubt so strong? I think that a great deal of it has to do with holding on to what we know and being consumed by the fear of what we don't know. We want to keep everything under control so that we will be "safe," although if we were honest with ourselves we would admit that no one has absolute control over anything. In the meantime, the judgment and criticism lurking in our heads paralyzes our actions before they even begin. I am beginning to see that it is not necessary to have the technique of painting under my belt before I attempt something. If I just experiment and watch what happens, I may stumble over something extraordinary and may even discover something no teacher thought to share with me.

Aiming for perfection is doomed to failure most of the time. I see this in how I try to care for guests. I pour so much effort into getting everything "perfect" that I am empty by the time each guest leaves (and, on occasion, even before the guest arrives). I have several friends who manage to entertain without all this fuss. It is not as though I am providing anything elaborate. It is the effort itself that is exhausting, and this is because it is loaded down with more than is required. This has nothing to do with whether I am enjoying the company or not. I almost always enjoy whoever is visiting me. The exhaustion comes from a combination of what goes into the preparation for a guest's arrival and what gets laid over this once he or she does arrive. There are activities that I don't think twice about, such as writing, editing, and cleaning. And then there are activities like painting and entertaining, activities where I suspect that I may be judged on my performance and I am unsure whether I can deliver. These are the fraught ones. My eye is always on the outcome, not on whatever is going on in that particular moment. I've never forgotten a visiting Englishman's response to some remark or other I had made. He looked at me and said, "Do you always keep score?"

I recently took a Chinese calligraphy workshop with Barbara Bash, whose flyer said that "the experience of calligraphy is about moving through space and leaving tracks behind. The brush is the most sensitive of the calligraphic tools, able to respond to the subtlest gesture." She told us that Cheng Man-Ching, a calligrapher, painter, poet, tai chi instructor, and doctor who taught in New York City for a decade before his death in 1974, was able to diagnose his students' ailments by studying their calligraphy. The brush reveals all.

At the end of the all-day workshop we taped great sheets of paper to the floor, and three people at a time prepared to use the Very Large Brushes made of horsehair. Kneeling before the empty page, each of us made a deep bow as we contemplated the unknown. I dipped my brush into the can, and, as I raised it, a thick ribbon of black ink sluiced off. I waited, listening, until the flood diminished to a trickle. Then the brush with its burden of ink made a great arc in the air and landed with a thud and a spatter before starting to swish across the paper. After which the brush lifted off and returned to the can. Another moment of contemplation, this time of the result. Then, almost before a claim of any kind could enter, another student folded the paper into four, stacked it in a pile with the others, and laid out a fresh sheet for the next person, thus emphasizing the impermanence of everything. We each acknowledged that we had allowed something to come through, and then we relinquished it.

Working with such big brushes was a revelation. There was no way we could control the outcome or what appeared on the page. This practice was not about perfection but about holding the intention to see what transpires. At the beginning there is anticipation, the energy gathers. This is the fuel. Then, as the brush moves, there is expansion. It happens. Finally, where the paint meets the paper, there is discovery.

I have been practicing meditation in one form or another for forty-five years, and I have been editing spiritual books for almost forty of those years, yet I have always been at a loss to describe what I mean by either "meditation" or "spirituality" when people not familiar with those terms ask. I don't know why it has been so difficult to articulate the very things that mean the most to me. As things have settled in my mind, I have realized that both these words describe the same thing. There are a great variety of meditation techniques, but the aim of all of them is to go beyond the technique. The most vivid image used to illustrate this is that of a small boat. You need the boat in order to cross the river, but once you arrive on the other side and walk on, it is not necessary to carry the boat on your back.

Meditation means being utterly present to what is going on, with no part of your mind split off or distracted by thoughts and sensations. Yes, thoughts and sensations will arise, but you are not consumed by them. You are not holding on to anything, nor are you held by anything. This is a state that few of us rest in for very long but it is where we feel at home once we are here. I was about to type "once we are there," which illustrates the problem perfectly. We think of meditation as being in a state that is somewhere other than *here*, a state that is hard to reach, that is not natural. Yet the opposite is true.

Now I have the answer for people who want to know what I mean by "spiritual books." They are books that help bring us to this natural state, by hook or by crook. We read about spirituality, we attend lectures, discussions, and workshops, we mull it all over, but these are largely intellectual pursuits. We give these ideas credence in our minds but do not put them into practice. This was beautifully explained by the Tibetan Buddhist teacher Tsoknyi Rinpoche, at the *Tricycle* conference on Buddhist practice at the World Trade Center in the summer of 2001.

"You can get to the World Trade Center in many different ways," he pointed out. "Helicopter, bicycle, subway, and so on, and from many directions, but all these methods of reaching the building are not the same as the actual experience of being here. This is the difference between knowledge and practice."

An Open Mind

I am awareness itself,
Bound only by my thirst for life.

ASHTAVAKRA GITA, *translated by Thomas Byrom*

 In the summer of 2003 I visited Japan for the first time. Soon after I returned, my friend Suzanne pressed upon me a book by Roland Barthes entitled *Empire of Signs.* I had always shied away from Barthes and his intellectualism, but I read this little volume in about twenty-four hours. Barthes had gone to Japan, where he was unable to understand the language, so that he could observe the culture without being influenced in any way by words. What he saw and recorded in the late 1960s coalesced my own reflections.

Here is Barthes's take on haiku (the Japanese poem form of three lines of 5, 7, and then 5 syllables). He describes it as "the apprehension of the thing as event, and not as substance." And again: "A faint plication [fold] by which is creased, with rapid touch, the page of life, the silk of language." A haiku reminds us that there are only essential moments. It records one such. Each poem is an ephemeral trace delicately preserved on the page in a drop of amber. It is visual rather than verbal. Like the Bible it uses few, if any, adjectives.

I think that perhaps the closest I have come to experiencing a haiku moment is this: as I emerged one day from the subway into the vast cathedral of New York's Grand Central Station, I sensed the shush of busy feet over its marble floors and was struck by the flood of light pouring through the great arched east window. I walked toward the place where the light fell on the floor in neat rectangles and just stood there for a little while in its radiance, feeling both bathed and blessed, as the morning commuters milled around me. I admit that on the page this is a little more than seventeen syllables, but in my memory there is just one luminous moment.

There were also two memorable moments in Japan. Kaz Tanahashi, a calligrapher, translator, writer, peace activist, and Zen teacher, and one of the leaders of the trip, took us to a favorite haunt in Kyoto, Gyoku-en, a tiny dessert shop adjacent to the Kamo River, at the north end of Pontocho. The little cafe had just four small tables but the most mouthwatering (literally) desserts we'd ever tasted—shaved ice with dark syrup. It was like gossamer and vanished on the tongue as soon as you started to savor it. The experience of *kaki-gori* in your mouth is like a moment of startling awareness followed by what happens once you begin to think about it. First the sense impression is just there, and then you label it "delicious." By this time you are at one remove or more from the experience itself. The commenting is a habit and occurs with such lightning speed it is hard to resist.

While in Kyoto we also paid a visit to Hashimoto Kansetsu's memorial museum and garden. Hashimoto was an early twentieth-century painter and master of tea ceremony who acquired this land when he was thirty and spent the rest of his life there painting and designing the lovely gardens and teahouses. We looked at the small museum of his paintings and wandered around the garden until it was time for whisked green *matcha* tea and dessert, which was offered to us very formally by two women from the Hashimoto family. I shall never forget the younger of the two. Each time she knelt to offer me some delicacy, she looked deep into my eyes and did not look away. I felt as though my very soul was being examined. No one has ever regarded me with such intensity. This was a level of engagement unprecedented anywhere in the world and particularly in a culture like that of Japan. I wondered if this was something she had been taught to do (which seemed unlikely) and what her reason was for doing it. Was it simply the desire to make a direct connection with anyone and everyone she encountered? I can still feel her great eyes holding me in their embrace.

It occurs to me that I am always trying to "seize the day." Most people interpret this to mean that they should grasp whatever is being offered them *now* because the opportunity might not arise again. But this is not really what it says. *Carpe diem* instructs us to take control and not let go. This is rather alarming. I would rather bring myself into the present as often as I can remember to, wait there, enjoy and appreciate what is happening, and then relinquish the experience when it is over.

The realization that this is how the universe works is a great help in taking care of the body, particularly if it is in pain. When I have a medical problem I let my mind rest in the area where my body is malfunctioning and, rather than fighting or rejecting what is there, I try to release it. I search for the edges of the disorder, whether it is a swelling, an eruption on the skin, or a muscle spasm, and then visualize them softening. Actually, it is less a visualization and more an experiencing. It is much better if you can feel the sensation in your body rather than trying to see it in your mind. I explain to my body that since whatever it is is made up of its own elements, I would like it to relinquish the form it has assumed and redistribute itself to wherever it was in the first place. Problems arise when things accumulate: matter, tensions, resentment, you name it. In the natural order of things, forms arise and then dissipate. Nothing stands still. Somehow we spend all our energy trying to keep a firm grip on things in an effort to control our surroundings.

Twenty-five years ago, when I developed a lump on the outside of my little finger, the doctor wanted me to have surgery to remove it, but I decided to try an experiment before I submitted to the knife. I couldn't bring myself to believe that I could get rid of the growth entirely through visualization, but each day on the subway I concentrated on it and encouraged it to disintegrate and return whence it came. I did this for a couple of months with no discernible result—and then my husband Neil walked out, never to return. I was, of course, devastated and completely distracted. I didn't think about my finger again for some time, and when I did, I discovered that the lump had dematerialized (literally). It has never returned.

In addition to grasping at images and experiences, we often keep locked in our minds desires that are so strong they govern our everyday behavior. Generally we hide this tendency from ourselves. On March 3, 2003, my mother died, and I flew to England for her funeral. The next day, although I was unaware of it at the time, the first copy of my book *Nothing Left Over* arrived at my apartment. I returned to New York after a week, and three days later I inherited a small plot in the community garden where I had been working for almost two years. In just ten days there had been a death, a birth, and an inheritance. I was regaling my friend David with this story, and he remarked that it seemed as though I had undergone a major shift. "So, do you think that after so long a man might come into my life?" I asked him. He laughed and said, "I think it is inevitable."

A few months later I told this story to another friend. She said, "You need to let go of any ideas you have about the kind of man who might arrive. Your fixed ideas of what a man should be like are a wall between you and whoever turns up." She was right, but her words came as a shock. There is no way to be open to whatever or whoever the universe brings you if you have already put in your order and are just waiting for it to be delivered.

I have no clear memory of learning how to read and write, type, ride a bicycle, drive a car, or do yoga, but I have become very curious about how these things took place. I remember that when I first attended a tai chi chuan class, I used to come home with a headache. I am aware that I shouldn't be interfering in the learning process of a physical movement with my head, my intellect, but I admit that that is what I generally do. I attempt to grasp the instructions and hang on for dear life, wanting to fix them in my memory like a dead butterfly pinned in a display case. Somehow I need to discover how to get from the basic principles to the natural movement and flow.

I am going to use my brushpainting lessons to see if I can catch a glimpse of how the process actually works. Up until now, each time I practice and see a perfect brush stroke on the page, I say, "Aha. There's one." But it's too late. What is in front of me is the result, not the act itself. With the next stroke I try to mimic perfection, but it is a failure because I have no idea what it is that I am trying to copy. I wasn't there at the moment when perfection happened. Perhaps, at the very moment when I was being shown how to paint that stroke, I was worrying that I wouldn't get it right and I laid a blanket of fear over what was going on. The blanket produced . . . a blank. The fear is what I conjure up when I try to practice because that is what I focused on at the moment of learning.

I don't want to practice doing something wrong because then I will become adept at doing it incorrectly. It is said that the difference between an amateur and a professional is that an amateur practices technique until she gets it right and a professional practices until she gets it right and then continues to practice it correctly until she doesn't get it wrong.

Like many people in the West, I want each movement of a new technique explained. There is a different attitude in Asia, where students watch what the teacher does and acquire the skill by copying the teacher's actions. There is almost no verbal instruction. I am beginning to suspect that words can obfuscate observation of what is actually going on. They are all commentary.

The best way to learn a language is to immerse yourself in it, to go and live in the country and absorb through your ears. As babies, we learned to crawl, walk, talk, and everything else through experimenting. Maybe such things never change?

What does the action feel like? What is the sensation? I need to shift my attention from the outcome, the result, to the activity itself. The result is like evidence in a crime. It can provide clues to what happened but only if you are looking in the right place and notice what is there. It is never as accurate or conclusive as being a witness at the time the crime was committed.

One method of improving your painting skill is to go to a museum and make a precise copy of a painting by an old master. But my attempts at copying are often a disaster. When I sit down with something like the classic seventeenth-century Chinese *Mustard Seed Garden Manual of Painting* or an example painted by a contemporary teacher, once I transfer my attention to the empty paper in front of me, all memory of what I have just looked at is wiped clean from my mind, as though I had never seen it. I have ruefully observed this again and again. Somewhere there is a block in my brain.

In painting, as in everything else, if you are always working for a result, then you are putting your life on hold. You can see the result in your mind, but it is in the future and hasn't happened yet. Or you can look back at what already took place, but that is the unrecapturable past. Pure presence is the answer.

Why is it that I am always drawn to the most arduous approach? Do I believe that anything difficult to achieve is worth more? Suppose I attempted something new and found it deliciously easy? There would be no more need for this mental girding of my loins, this tension I carry everywhere I go. In many unfortunate ways, I am wired. This is probably the reason I have never been able to float. I cannot entrust myself to the water. It undoubtedly has to do with my ridiculous desire to exert control over everything. All around me I see people and things falling apart, and there is really nothing I can do to prevent this, so why do I continue to believe I can stop the same thing from happening to me?

Sometime long ago I gained the impression that if I understood the mechanics of the universe (or at least my small corner of it) I would be able to harness the forces of creation and work with them rather than against them, and stop trying to do things in ways they cannot be done. I am a very law-abiding citizen. But when I discover that a rule or simple procedure has changed and no one has seen fit to advise me, it is hard for me to stay calm and take this new development in my stride.

I usually manage to avoid turmoil in my life but sometimes the slightest threat can throw me into a tizzy. Not that I fall apart, but I do experience a fluttering in my gut. Oh how jealously I try to guard the status quo! I always want to be the person who decides on change. I don't want it to happen without my consent. Yes, I know that the only constant in this world is change, but apparently I consider myself exempt from this universal law. Instead of learning how to ride the crests of the waves, I continue to cower in my little boat as it gets tossed back and forth. No wonder I have such a queasy ride.

One habit has me firmly in its grip (and I am not alone): I am always leaning into the next moment in an effort to complete what I am doing. This, of course, keeps me permanently off balance. I sit down to write something, and my mind is immediately bent on finishing it, wanting it to be done already, rather than enjoying the experience itself, which will never ever be repeated. Writing this page is a once-in-a-lifetime happening, as is anything and everything. Yet I am almost never present to what is happening. Since the world doesn't stand still, if I keep going, I will inevitably get to the end. There's no need to try to get there early.

We live our lives as though whatever we want might arrive in the very next moment. We are skeptical about it arriving right now, but if we could just get to the end of this (whatever "this" happens to be), there is a strong possibility that we might be happy. I have observed this even in periods of meditation: I sit down on my cushion, look at my watch to see the time, and set my internal alarm clock for half an hour, as though the point of the meditation is to get to the end of the

32

half-hour rather than to be present in each moment. But the point is *not* to get to the future or to be able to say that I have spent half an hour on my cushion.

I was once taught "Don't work for results," and my initial reaction was "If you don't work for results, you won't get any." At the time I was helping to renovate a brownstone and, indeed, we never seemed able to finish even one part of the house. I see now that the answer lies in having an end in mind but not focusing on it to the exclusion of the activity itself. For instance, when I get on the subway, I make sure to get on the right train and get off at the appropriate stop, but I don't focus on where and when I will leave the train while I am sitting there. It is certainly at the back of my mind, but it doesn't receive 99 percent of my attention.

Our reluctance to remain in the present comes from our natural restlessness. We want to find tranquillity and fulfillment, and for some strange reason we believe that we have to go elsewhere to discover it.

The Availability of Angels

... once in a while, I have chanced, among the quick
things, upon the immutable.

What more could one ask?

"Have You Ever Tried to Enter the Long
Black Branches?," *Mary Oliver*

 If you consider how unaware most
of us are almost all the time, it is a
miracle that the world still functions as well as it does. It is not
that we have the odd moment of inattention. What we
have are infrequent moments of attention, and these
moments are very fleeting. Isn't this is a little scary?

For instance, a few days ago, I put two eggs in a
saucepan, added cold water, lit the flame beneath it,
and returned to the computer. I have forgotten what
was happening in the kitchen several times and remembered only when my nose registered a strong
smell of burning. I decided to prevent this from oc-
curring again. I wrote EGGS on a little yellow sticker,

put it right on the computer screen, and relaxed. A few minutes later, I decided that what I really needed was some fresh air and exercise, and I set off for the garden a few blocks away. When I returned half an hour later, I just managed to avert disaster in the kitchen, but the eggs were very hardboiled. The yellow sticker with its reminder was still happily affixed to the screen, but, of course, I had not been there to see it. How could I have had the eggs so firmly in mind one minute and then lost that connection completely?

It is often hard to believe just how un-present we can be. As I was getting out of the bath one day, I noticed a large red splotch on the inside of my wrist and next to it two small scratches. I was bewildered. What had I done to my arm and when had this happened? My mind raced around for clues. Perhaps I had been putting undue pressure on it while I was asleep? But that didn't explain the scratches. I had been on my knees gardening the afternoon before. Maybe I was allergic to some plant I had touched or had been stung by an insect? I had also been to visit two small boys for a play date. Had there been a moment when I had banged into something in their apartment as I endeavored to prevent an accident? If any of these things had taken place, I certainly hadn't been aware of it at the time. Three or four days later the marks vanished, and I didn't even notice their departure.

Revelations often come to me in the bath. At the end of one rather long day during my time in Japan, I decided to bathe before dinner. As I entered the hot tub, I realized that when I had shed my clothes in my room, I hadn't been wearing my money belt (which also contained my passport and traveler's checks) although I knew for certain that I had been wearing it when I set off in the morning. We had been gone for eight hours, and somewhere along the way it had disappeared. My stomach lurched, but I decided not to panic—yet. However, there was no way I could relax and enjoy the bubbling water, so I climbed out and returned to my room to double-check. The money belt was lying on my futon. I remembered taking off my watch and earrings, and then my clothes, but had blanked out when it came to the money belt. Immensely relieved, I returned to the hot bath and soaked there for a long time.

Such moments of absence are devastating. I thought back to the time near the end of a nine-day silent retreat with meditation teacher Toni Packer when I had held my coffee filter under the hot-water urn and the scalding water had streamed through onto my toes. After seven days of practicing being present, I had done something I'd never done when I wasn't practicing: I had failed to put a cup under the filter!

In Japan, I realized that during the day, when it seemed as though there was nothing to do or I didn't want to participate in what most of the others were doing—visiting an exhibit of modern painting, buying snacks or soft drinks, going to a shrine, or chanting at the tomb of a revered teacher—I had tuned out rather than remaining aware of my surroundings. I had removed myself from the scene. So there is this stubborn "absent[ing myself] from felicity awhile" (Hamlet) in addition to the natural tendency of the mind to drift off.

In April the first pear blossoms appeared on the bare trees outside my window, and when I saw them they brought a smile to my heart. These blossoms bring such white beauty to our city streets. A day later I noticed that I was no longer seeing them. I had already started taking their glory for granted, even though they would be soon be gone for another year. Then the temperature soared to the midnineties for three days and suddenly all the blossoms had gone, so I never got another chance to appreciate them.

There is another side to this. In the last few years I have become addicted to orchids. It's not unusual. Many people who are given an orchid for a special occasion soon find themselves peering longingly into florists' windows. Then they start to attend orchid shows and never look back. This year I brought home three exquisite plants from an annual show. Several times a day I wander over to the table by the window where I have placed the orchids and gaze at them hungrily. In some not so subtle way I am doing my best to possess them. I am trying to drink in the experience of seeing them and imprint it in my memory, knowing full well that these orchids may never flower again.

Orchids can be temperamental when you don't grow them in greenhouses, with special lights, or have a jungle in your backyard. Sometimes they seem to acclimatize themselves to your living conditions, the blooms last six weeks, and then a few months later there are more. But just as often, orchids take umbrage at a change in atmosphere, their buds drop off, and they go on strike. I treat all newcomers to my home the same way and can never tell which ones will thrive and which will go the way of all flesh. Perhaps it is because their presence here is so tenuous that I don't regard orchids in the same way as the blossom on the trees, which I assume will return next year and the year after. On reflection, both attitudes are best surrendered. In the case of the pear blossoms, I have no guarantee that they will be here next year or even next week. I don't even know whether *I* will be here at those times. Nothing in this world is certain. In the case of the orchids, there is no way I can possess either them or their images. We must neither turn away nor imagine that we can hold on to things. All we can do is behold these wondrous forms of nature and be glad.

One day I attended a concert and my gaze fell on a man seated a few rows in front of me. All I could see was the back of his head, but instantly I was transported back to a time when I was dating a handsome youth who had the same bone structure and held his head at the same angle. I could see his smile and remember the way he held me in his arms on the dance floor. Later in the evening my mind roved through all the men I had dated in those early days and I tried to recall each of their names. One name escaped me until I was about to fall asleep, but I was amazed and amused to watch all these men parade through my mind and realize that they had been lurking there all along, held in memory and forever young. For each one there was a particular moment I remembered, and the rest of our time together had been lost—or so it seemed. What makes some moments indelible and others slip away like water through a sieve?

I have been saying kaddish for my mother early in the morning as I sit in my high-backed yellow armchair in the corner by the window, and as I do so, one image of her arises. She is almost at the end of her life and is also sitting in a big armchair, searching with difficulty for the right words to express what she wants to say, and smiling when she cannot manage it. She turns to me and asks whether I think that she is the youngest in the senior home (she is eighty-nine). I reply that I can't tell because I don't know the ages of all the others and it would be rude of me to ask them. "You mean all these crematoria," she says as she glances around the room at all the elderly folk. "Crematoria?" I am stunned. "Do you mean 'old people'?" I ask gently. "Yes, of course that's what I mean," she says.

In addition, I can conjure her up many years earlier standing at the kitchen sink of the house where we were living when I left for the United States in my twenties. Try as I might, I cannot find all those other snapshots I thought were lodged in my memory box. Nan was a vivacious and wonderful woman, but I cannot produce many instances of these qualities or any moments when the two of us were particularly close, even though I always considered her to be my best friend. What was it about the quality of my attention that etched those two moments so sharply in my mind?

The firing mechanism in our brains seems so mercurial. Even now, when I want to remember a particular moment and tell myself firmly that I don't want to lose this feeling or image, the instruction doesn't take hold. Or, rather, what I remember later is the instruction to remember rather than the moment itself.

Toward the end of her life when her mind was no longer what it once had been, my mother began saying "Bless you, bless you," to those around her each time they did something to help. I used to joke with her that perhaps she should change her name to Saint Nan. I realized recently that I have inherited this rather nice habit. Very often now, instead of saying "Thank you," I say "Bless you," and people appreciate it much, much more. Last week, for instance, someone responded, "I could use a blessing."

There has been a real change in my life in the year since Nan died. I have shifted the emphasis of my work and am now more open to anything that comes along. I have made several good new friends. I am taking three different classes. I am starting to enjoy life. I am full of hope. So much seems to be opening up for me now. I feel like a child with boxes of toys all lined up on the shelf who has never raised her eyes from the floor until now, when she takes the boxes down one at a time, and starts to explore. I don't know how to explain this but perhaps it has something to do with the fact that, even though I was living three thousand miles away, for the last ten years of her life I felt more like my mother's parent than her child. Now this great responsibility has been lifted, and I am beginning to play.

One such occasion was a lovely day I spent in the spring sunshine with my friend Natasha at the New York Botanical Garden, in the Bronx. We went there primarily to see the exhibit of spectacular orchid blooms in the conservatory, but afterward we wandered through the grounds with the book on New York trees I had bought the week before at a talk by the author, where I had learned, among other extraordinary facts, that New York City is home to over 5 million trees.

I have always had a great affinity for trees. In fact, when I was a teenager, and my name was Toinette Rees (T. Rees), I would often sign my name with five primitively drawn trees, with a period after the first one. Yet it has taken me until now to focus on individual trees and come to a fuller realization of this affinity.

There are acres of trees at the New York Botanical Garden. The first time I went there, I was disappointed that that there were so many more trees than flowers. For me, a botanical garden implies a profusion of flowers. Trees, yes, but in the background. So on that visit I hardly noticed the trees. This time everything was different.

The individual trees in the garden have small identification labels with English and Latin names and country of origin, and there are varieties from all over the world. I found myself running up hills, creeping under canopies of branches, peering around huge trunks, meeting the trees themselves on a truly intimate level. After all these years, we were finally getting to know one another.

Since it was mid-March, each tree was bare of leaves, although some were showing their first red-tinged buds. The first one to welcome us was a white-barked Himalayan birch, whose softly curved branches resembled waving arms. For some reason, its dried catkins from the previous autumn stuck up rather than hanging down.

Then came a great black pine. Most of its lower branches bent toward the ground, as though the weight of years, or perhaps snow, had been too much for them to bear. But near the crown some branches were reaching up while others stretched down, as though they couldn't agree on the right direction.

Around a bend in the path we came to a Japanese flowering cherry. It was so low to the ground it gave the impression that its branches were kneeling on the earth. Maybe it had miscalculated how high it needed to grow before it began to grow branches of that length?

Our next encounter was with a river birch, her (definitely *her*) roots sunk in a pool of accumulated water that we squelched through to get close enough to examine the bark peeling off the trunk in handfuls, as though she was in a continuous state of undress.

Another beauty was the Japanese stewartia (most of these names were new to me, and perhaps to you) whose twisted trunk of peeling bark revealed layers of ochre, deep rose, and slate, a kind of elegant camouflage, as though tooled in marble. And this tree was rivaled by a sturdy lacebark pine with equally beautiful dappled bark in more muted tones.

Down by the clear and turbulent Bronx River, we encountered a tree in full sunlight that had burst into leaf, despite the fact that we had had a major snowfall about two weeks before. I smiled, acknowledging how I too am always early for appointments. However hard I try to arrive late, I fail miserably. I must share some genes with this tree.

The other wonderful moments of our day came

when we saw a large butterfly alight on a rock and when we stood and drank in the song of a cardinal perched at the top of a tree celebrating the arrival of spring.

I spent all that evening immersed in books on trees and making plans to visit other New York parks with a sketchbook so that I could get to know these other inhabitants of the city better, marveling that attending one lecture could have such an influence on my life.

For the last few months I have been using a bookmark without focusing on the words printed on it. One morning, out of the blue, I finally read what it said: "'Angels from the Lord lead and protect us every moment.'—Emanuel Swedenborg." All my life I have been very resistant to the idea of angels, especially their wings, harps, and sweet expressions. I don't subscribe to the notion that there is an entity out, up, or even down there orchestrating everything in the universe, but I have certainly been puzzled by all the reported activity of angels.

In the Old Testament the Hebrew word translated as "angel" is *malach*, which means "messenger." Perhaps angels are an instant messaging service? You can receive their messages only if you are there and if you are willing to accept them. These messages are ephemeral, and if they are not welcomed in the moment, they vanish, leaving no trace. Messages from the universe are always arriving, but they are rarely received. Most people ignore them most of the time. Right now I am sitting by an open window. The morning sun has just slipped above the top of the tree outside, and the play of light and wind through the net curtains stencils a shimmering pattern of luminescence on the dark green fabric of the sofa. The golden strands and black diamond shadows flare and shift and disappear again and again. After a few minutes, the sun goes behind a cloud and the magic show is over. It turns out that the answer to that enigmatic question about whether there is a crash in the forest when a tree falls and there is no one to hear it is *yes*. Trees are always crashing and light is always dancing, even though we are not always either listening or watching.

So many coincidences have occurred in my life that I don't know what to make of the phenomenon. What draws these skeins of my life together so intricately?

The most extraordinary example happened a few years back when my son Adam was moving into an apartment at college and I was accumulating all the stuff he might need. The one thing I didn't seem to have available was a spare garbage can for his kitchen and so, early one Sunday morning while he was still asleep, I set off for a store where I thought I would find a good one. My mission was unsuccessful, but on the way back I decided to stop and treat myself to a caffe latte—something I would not normally do if I was alone. As I entered the cafe, I saw that ahead of me in the line was a woman wearing a deep blue silk *shalwar kameez*, the traditional Punjabi tunic and pants in which so many Indian and Pakistani women look both elegant and comfortable. I love to wear a shalwar kameez at home, but I do not often do so in the street; however, on this particular morning, that was what I too was wearing.

All my shalwar kameezes have been bought in India, and I have never found a source in this country for the cotton ones I prefer. I decided that if the woman was still there when I was ready to leave, I would ask her where she had purchased hers, so that at last I would not have to travel halfway around the world or send emissaries to do my shopping. When I sat down with my coffee I noticed that she was just two tables away. We looked at each other and then away, but when she got up to get a plastic knife for her bagel, she came over and spoke to me. She was intrigued by the fact that I was dressed as she was.

47

I told her that I had been planning to come and talk to her about this, and very soon she was sitting at my table. She told me that she had, in fact, bought her shalwar kameez in Lahore, Pakistan, where she lived. She was visiting her daughter, who lived one block from me. Her daughter and son-in-law were still asleep, and she, like me, had gone out to purchase a garbage can for them at the same store! We smiled. She asked me if I had ever been to Pakistan, and I told her that I had once visited India but not yet Pakistan. However, it was because of a Pakistani woman that I had come to the United States in the first place. I launched into the story of the three Pakistani girls, two of whom had attended boarding school with me in England, how the one who was my friend and now lived with her French husband outside Washington, D.C., had invited me to the United States in 1963 to visit her and that it was during that visit that I had met the man I eventually came to work for. The second sister, I recounted, had become a doctor and gone to live in Norway, where she had married another doctor, and they were currently working in Pakistan. The third sister had never married. She had remained in Pakistan and become a journalist. My companion interrupted me: "You are talking about Riffy," she said. I stopped in my tracks. "How do you know her name?" I asked. I had given only the first names of the two sisters who had attended high school with me. She told me that she had met Rifaat in kindergarten, that they had remained friends all these years, and that they lived not far from one another in Lahore. We were both a little stunned. All these coincidences were beyond the ordinary.

In 2002 I made a trip to Montana, having yearned for many years to see Big Sky Country. Judy, the friend I was visiting, lives in Bitterroot Valley, in the southeast of the state. As in much of rural America, mailboxes are bunched together where a lane joins a more major road. Apart from Judy I knew only two people in Montana. One died some years back, and the other is Therese Schroeder-Sheker, a harpist who plays her instrument and sings to the dying at the hospital in Missoula, where she teaches music thanatology. The first time I heard Therese play was at a conference for nurses, and her pure, husky voice, the sound of her harp, and the story of how she started caring for the dying moved me to tears. She and I attended another workshop that followed hers, and we both hated it so much we stole out after about ten minutes and had a meal together instead. It turned out that she couldn't transport her relatively small wooden traveling harp on public transportation and had to rent a stretch limo wherever she went. She offered to give me a ride into New York, and we lurched around in the back of the limo (I had never imagined how uncomfortable riding in one of these can be. It yaws as you turn the corner) while we exchanged life stories. We remained in touch for several years in the hope of doing a book together, but it never quite worked out. The first time we drew up at the mailboxes, I was stunned to see that she was a neighbor of Judy's. Judy had never met her but was aware that she lived on the same road.

On my last full day in Montana, we drove south over Chief Joseph Pass—and through the tall, slender, dark green Douglas firs and lodgepole pines needling the heavens as far as the eye could see—to Big Hole National Battlefield, where in 1877 ninety Nez Perce Indians and twenty-seven white settlers killed each other. Early in the afternoon we pressed on to the Jackson Hot Springs Lodge for lunch. Inside was a great hall built with pine logs, a huge fireplace, a balcony all the way around, and moose heads and antlers in all the appropriate places. While we were waiting for our sandwiches and microbrew to arrive, Judy discovered a back issue of *Montana Living* on a little table. The lodge had been written up, and she wanted to me to see what the magazine had to say about it. I began to read the piece and was astonished to discover that the lodge had been built by the only other person I had known in Montana, Dorothea Dooling. She had arrived there fifty years earlier, fallen in love with a rancher, married him, and stayed to raise her family. I had met Doro over twenty-five years ago when she founded *Parabola* magazine in New York City.

I sometimes wonder about the trajectory of our lives, but perhaps it is not as arbitrary as it often appears. Since "angels" are always available to us, it is up to us to recognize this and take advantage of what they have to offer sooner rather than later. I am beginning to think that if we hone our attention and become more aware of the things that matter, we can glimpse more in creation than is normally visible to us. We admit on some level that everything is connected, that there are no real edges to people and things, but we are so busy throwing up protective barriers between ourselves and everything else ("I will go thus far but no further") that we are usually blind to the great web of possibilities that surrounds us. Occasionally we let down our guard, the walls become a little transparent, and what seems like a miracle occurs. It isn't really a miracle, but it seems that way to us because most of the time we don't allow ourselves to see what is there in front of us.

There is an illuminating poem by Wislawa Szymborska called "Love at First Sight," in which she speculates about the number of times our lives may have touched those of the man or woman we eventually fall in love with. Our luggage might have been adjacent to theirs at an airport, or maybe they held a door open for us somewhere without our knowing it—

Perhaps a "sorry" muttered in a crowd?
A curt "wrong number" caught in the receiver?

When I think about coincidence in this way, I understand that, given how old some of us are, how much we travel, and how many people we have come into contact with, there are thousands of ways we are, undoubtedly, all connected. But we are missing most of these connections. In future I vow to keep my eyes wide open.

Surrender

> In truth, everything arises in order to disappear; everything we have, everything we think we are, must at some point be surrendered, for it is only on loan from the bounty of the Divine.
>
> Alistair Shearer, *in his introduction to the* Mundaka Upanishad

 The gesture of surrender has been much on my mind. It seems that everywhere I turn, the subject arises—in my reading, in my correspondence, in my daily experience.

One of the things I managed to surrender the other day was the idea that I couldn't paint, that I was kidding myself if I thought there was any possibility of ever being any good at brushpainting. For the first time I just sat there and watched as a branch with two deep orange persimmons, then a scarlet poppy, a spray of deep pink magnolia, and a delicate Japanese chrysanthemum appeared before me on the sheets of paper. I was quite startled by the results. Several of the paintings were worth keeping (I usually consign everything to the wastebasket without a second thought). I didn't quite understand what was different on that day, but I had the impression that some of the technique had made its way into my system and so I was no longer worrying that I was not making the strokes correctly.

Yet the following day, and the one after that, the proficiency had vanished. I worked with different brushes, different papers, different strokes—all to no avail. Perhaps I was trying too hard to relax (obviously a contradiction in terms) but it certainly didn't seem that way. What a puzzlement. I just watched what was going on and claimed neither the triumph nor the defeat. Maybe it is like meditation and other disciplines: you keep plodding along, doing the best you can, starting fresh each time, and then, one day, there is a shift, a quantum leap. Or not. The principal of the English boarding school I attended used to say that there was a certain merit in just showing up (she was speaking about going to church, but surely this applies to any activity). And the composer Philip Glass once remarked that if he doesn't sit down at the piano every day, he won't be there when the music finally arrives.

Sometimes, when we experience particular resistance to an idea we need to understand, the rug is pulled out from under our feet, and we no longer have any choice but acceptance. In the summer of 2001 I made a pilgrimage to Konya, the city in western Turkey where the thirteenth-century mystic poet Rumi lived most of his life and where he found and then lost his beloved friend and teacher, Shems-i-Tabriz.

I should explain that I am not someone who is comfortable with full prostrations, be they Buddhist or Muslim. At Shems's tomb (he was murdered and his body never found, but this is the place where his coffin stands and where he is eternally remembered) I prostrated myself with the other women, but it made me uneasy. Later in the day, when we returned to our hotel, I missed my footing on the two low steps at the entrance to the restaurant. Before I knew it I had been catapulted face down on the ground and could not get up.

People rushed to my aid and carried me to a chair. Quantities of ice arrived, someone administered jin shin jitsu, and our ever-cheerful bus driver, who spoke no English, sat beside me and held my hand in his firm grasp. I had never had an accident in my life, and here I was completely immobile. People were asking if I thought I'd broken any bones and whether a doctor should be called. Since I was able to wiggle my toes, I didn't think anything could be broken, and I assumed that it was just a bad sprain, which only rest and time would heal, so I didn't opt for a doctor. What I really wanted was a strong Scotch, but this was impossible because the hotel was strictly Muslim and therefore dry. My whole system had received such a violent shock that my torso shuddered for about ten minutes. I drank two entire bottles of water instead of the longed-for whiskey.

After dinner (to which I was carried by our driver and our guide), five dervishes arrived to give us a private demonstration of "turning" or "whirling." As I sat watching them, it came to me that Shems, or perhaps Rumi, had heard what was reverberating in my mind and had responded: "You don't like to humble yourself before Allah? Who cares what you like or don't like? Down you go without more ado." I had, it seemed, finally got my "come-downance." I am reluctant to participate in rituals, and the evening promised to be one where we were expected to join in and learn how to do *zikr*, or "remembrance of God." I observed rather ruefully that it was amazing the lengths I was willing to go to, to avoid surrender and give up the tight control I try to exercise over myself all the time! Yet wasn't the whole point of the pilgrimage to Turkey (and, indeed, of my life) the remembrance of God?

The usual interpretation of "Islam" is "surrender," and the implication is that the surrender is to God. But in his novel *Abandon*, Pico Iyer describes how, if you see surrender in terms of a surrendering *of* rather than surrendering *to*, it becomes clear that what has to be given up is *everything*. We are such nitpickers—perhaps willing to give up this or that (for now, but probably not forever). But giving up *everything*? This is a tall order. When I was taught Transcendental Meditation, someone told me that nothing should come between you and the Divine, not even a mantra. Eventually even the mantra must be surrendered for there to be complete union. In India, around the third century B.C., the sage Patanjali wrote in his *Yoga Sutras* of *aparigraha*, or "not grasping or claiming," and of *ishvarapranidhana*, or "surrender to the Lord," two requisites, he said, for living a life of purity and devotion. Later, these ideas of nonattachment were developed by the Buddha. The question is what do they mean for us in the twenty-first century? The basic human condition has not changed, however much loot we have accumulated in our closets, our minds, and our hearts. How can we divest ourselves of all that we cling to in each and every moment of our lives?

Perhaps we can start in small ways and then raise the bar. For instance, I am in the enviable position of being a New Yorker with a spare sofabed, and so from time to time I find myself with a guest. Each time this happens I am faced with the problem of accommodating a friend and enjoying the warmth and energy of her (generally) companionship, juxtaposed with the fact that she is sleeping in my office and placing off limits all that I need to do in there. Hospitality dictates that I cannot disturb her at the time I like to turn on my computer and check my e-mail first thing in the day. When you welcome someone into your home, that person comes as a package—with the possibility of fun and companionship but also the full complement of idiosyncrasies and inconvenience. It is Saturday morning, and I have done all my early morning chores, in addition to making a trip to the bank. It's 9 A.M. and still there is no sign that she is awake. Resentment starts to well up inside me, and then I realize that this is just another variation on learning to accept things the way they are and not continually expecting or wishing them to be some other way.

Since my morning routine runs almost by itself, a jolt like this gives me the chance to come to, reevaluate the situation, and discover what else there is to do right now. Life moves forward inexorably, never missing a beat. It is rather like water overflowing: if you block it on one side, it will escape elsewhere. So now I find myself with my legs up on the sofa, writing this paragraph about my state of mind, and admitting that a disruption of the normal flow and a change of direction is not necessarily a bad thing. Particularly if I can drop any trace of resentment I may be harboring about the behavior of the universe (or my guest).

All you can offer to another person is yourself. You don't truly own anything else. When you make a sacrifice, what you are really offering up is yourself. The object you are sacrificing is a symbol, a gesture, and so if you do not relinquish yourself in the moment of sacrifice, then the gesture is empty.

I was reading about sacrifices of atonement at the Temple in Jerusalem in Adin Steinsaltz's book *The Essential Talmud.* I had not understood before that, according to the sages, such sacrifices could be offered only in expiation of sins committed inadvertently. Crimes committed deliberately were not redeemable through sacrifice. Furthermore, a sacrifice could be offered only by someone who had already voiced remorse. The offering was seen not as a substitute for penitence, or as a punishment, but as an opportunity for the sinner to sacrifice himself to God, that is, rededicate himself to the Divine. The offering at the altar and sacrifice there was a substitute for the life of the person who brought it, since by his negligence, the sinner now owed his life to the Creator and was required to offer it back to Him. This is a very different view of sacrifice from the one held by most people today.

Rededication is always a good idea, whether we believe that we have transgressed or not. Our attention is so spotty that there is bound to be much that we have overlooked. Becoming aware of that and vowing to try to do better can never hurt.

I noticed one evening that I was treating an elderly and rather deaf dinner guest as an object and not a person. I did not truly engage with her, and that was sad. If you invite someone into your home, surely the whole point is to connect with her, not avoid her. Everyone wants to connect deeply with others. It may be difficult for a meeting to take place because the other person is as hidden as I am, but if I don't make an effort, why do I expect the other person to come through? It is up to me to make the first move on every occasion. It is the least I can offer.

When I am with my friend Susan, what I often experience is delight. I think that the two of us meet on such a direct level because we are both rather unadorned people. We say what we mean and don't mince words. When I am with her, I feel as though she is completely there for me and I suspect that she feels the same way. I am so lucky to have her in my life. She was a friend of my husband Neil, and I found it impossible to reach out to her while he was alive because he stayed briefly in her apartment on the Lower East Side after he left me. But his death in 1989 drew Susan and me together. As she once wrote to me, "One of the greatest gifts of Neil's illness and death has been the connections I have made with the other people in his constellation, as though in some way highly idiosyncratic of Neil, we are his legacies to one another. And though we are not necessarily bound to one another for all time, we have all been reacquainted with ourselves, with one another, and with Neil, through Neil. I am glad that this effect on me has included you."

I suppose that it is only when we are willing to drop our guard and stop trying to protect ourselves (Whatever that means—what is it that we are trying to protect?) that we can meet other people on this level. When this happens, the doing and the knowing that we espouse during most of our waking hours become more transparent, and we can see through them to what is real.

When Susan gives her attention, she gives it whole-heartedly. If you are with someone like that, then it frees you to reciprocate. It has to do with holding nothing back for oneself. No self-referencing, no commenting, no preparing what you are going to say next. Her friendship is a priceless treasure. Armed with the knowledge of how it is between us, I shall try to put the same thing into practice with others I know less well and with whom I have never shared this approach.

I received a phone call recently from Sophie Wilkins, an editor who worked with me at Knopf in the late 1960s and early 1970s and whom I had encountered at a memorial service the previous week. Years ago she and I had formed a mutual admiration society because I had been amazed that she was able to find so much to say in her reader's reports about each manuscript she read (she went into great detail for at least a page and a half), while she marveled at my ability to write no more than two or three sentences. Since that time we had each lived our lives true to form—she expansively and I economically.

When I met Sophie a week later for lunch it was

hard to believe that she was now eighty-eight, and I detected no visible change in her. She was still the same intense but charming Viennese woman, word-smith, and almost-ingénue that I remembered. Each of us still saw something in the makeup of the other that was a cause for wonder and celebration. It is not that we envied each other, but we felt the urge to ap-plaud what we saw, and neither of us was abashed to admit it. All of us are so different from one another, and there must be all kinds of things to admire in other people if we really looked, traits that comple-ment our own. Yet instead of applauding the good that we see, we often criticize the aspects that we don't like, the reflection of elements in our own char-acter that we hide from ourselves but that are as clear as day to everyone else.

Not long ago I attended a reading at a local book-store. Afterward I told the salesclerk that I could no longer find any copies of my book, which had been out on the table from publication in April until mid-October. I wanted to know if they still had any in stock. He asked me the title so that he could check in the computer, and I drew a blank. I decided not to panic, and eventually the title did float back into my mind and I was able to give him the information. I don't know what he made of my aberration, and

I myself am not sure whether to construe it as an instance of complete surrender or the early onset of Alzheimer's.

Just one year after I inherited my little plot of land in Riverside Park I was faced with a big decision. When I was first offered space in the community garden, it turned out to be a skinny strip and I was somewhat taken aback: it was only eleven by four and a half feet and was squeezed between an iron railing and the grating over the railroad. I had never even noticed this strip since I had been eyeing the twenty or so squarish plots that extended north and south in the median of the promenade. I took myself to the park to have a look at it. I had been on the waiting list for a long time, and I certainly didn't want to say no, but . . . In the end I asked whether, if I accepted this garden, I could have first refusal of the next plot that became available, and the board graciously agreed.

For twelve months I weeded, planted, watered, and generally tended this scrap of earth and grew very fond of it. Many of the other gardeners gave me plants from their gardens—both pink and cream lilies of the valley, yellow irises, a mauve rose of Sharon, ferns, and passionflower vines. In the spring it was a mass of purple, saffron, and striped crocuses, many of which I had planted in the fall. The blue parrot tulips thrust toward the sun, the ornamental onion spikes appeared, the scarlet poppy's furry gray leaves unfurled, and all the columbines were getting a head start. The growth was almost tangible. You could almost hear it thrum. I had ordered miniature hollyhocks, Japanese anemones, and alpine auriculas to arrive in mid-May to fill in the gaps I had noticed as I knelt there during the year, and I was all ready to sow pansy and nasturtium seeds once the weather was a little warmer.

Then I received a call offering me the chance to take over one of the squarish plots. I was given three days to make up my mind. The thought of losing all I had put into my first patch was painful. So much of myself had been invested. The following day, in the bitter wind, I walked over to the garden and inspected the section that was now available. At that time of year it was hard to tell what might be lurking under the ground. There weren't many bulbs coming up, but there was a beautiful rosebush surrounded by a small circle of paving stones, perhaps a hydrangea, and lots of plants that I didn't recognize at all. Certainly, the shape of the plot would allow for landscaping, while something only just over four feet wide (or perhaps I should say narrow) did not.

I returned home no surer about what my decision should be. But after I had talked with Rosemary, one of the other gardeners who was familiar with the new plot, I began to understand the nature of the decision I needed to make. Yes, I had put a great deal into "my" garden, but I wouldn't be losing anything by giving it up. The garden itself wasn't going to vanish. It would always be just a few yards away. I could appreciate and enjoy it every time I passed by. And I would be able to make someone else a gift of all that I had done there, relinquish my claim, and move on to love another patch of earth. I saw what had been holding me back was the thought of what I deserved for all the time, money, and effort I had put into the garden. In truth, I was lucky that now I wouldn't have the chance to become even more entrenched there. I could start fresh a few yards south and, with any luck, not get caught that way again. I decided to say yes to the new garden and vowed to care for it so that it would be a place of beauty for other people and not just myself. I would dedicate my work there to all the passersby—the joggers, the roller bladers, the cyclists, those who stroll past and those who lean over the fence and tell you what a joy this place is. In future I will remember that it is *their* garden that I'm working in, not my own.

Free Flow

Our society is very result-oriented; that's why we are so competitive. We are always stressed because we are always looking at something in the distance. If you are always looking at the top of the mountain you are climbing, you cannot be aware of the grass and flowers growing at your feet.

REFLECTIONS ON A MOUNTAIN LAKE,
Ani Tenzin Palmo

 This morning I understood the message the universe has been sending these last few months. It is hard to believe that I have been so obtuse. For so long I have wanted to leave the world of work (not irrevocably) and enter the world of play. Play has always seemed so unavailable to me, and the first step was to learn how to relax. After many years of practicing meditative techniques, you would think I would have grasped the principles of relaxation,

and—on one level—this is true. But it doesn't mean that I put it into practice as often as I would like to.

All this is taking place against a backdrop of very little work coming in. I haven't been feeling desperate about the lack of income, just rather disconcerted. This morning I realized that this must be the moment to focus on enjoying play and not work. I had wanted to learn to play, and I am finally being forced to make good on my desire, since there is no editing to distract me.

I now have all these other things that I would like to fit into my day: yoga, meditation, reading scripture, drawing and painting flowers, tai chi chuan, writing, a walk outside, seeing someone else, or going somewhere. How to proceed calmly so that these activities complement each other without my having the sensation that I cannot squeeze them all in? Each of these activities needs to be open-ended. I don't want to limit what might happen with any of them by setting a particular length of time for each. I don't do that with my editorial work, so why even consider doing it with the things I want to do more than work? Also I don't set a time to begin editing; I just do it when it is the right moment. So: I have to look more carefully and catch the right moment for each of these activities. I must stay open and not try to fix things either in my mind or my schedule.

I am also still rushing around trying to take care of every last detail before I'm willing to do any spiritual exercise. I feel that I have to clear my mental and emotional decks before something like presence can happen. Should I put spiritual discipline first, as I have always been advised? Or should I surrender the method I have tried to espouse for the last couple of years—leaving things to chance? A conundrum. What is the middle path here? How to balance my sanity and comfort with what I know needs to be done and am certain will bring the equanimity and enjoyment I crave so dearly? Is there some other approach I am just overlooking?

Even my scripture reading in the morning has turned into a competition. I set myself a goal of so many pages and then grimly hold myself to it. I don't just see what arises in my mind in response to the material or consider going deeper into a particular sentence. No, it's on to the future. Must reach the horizon before it is too late. Racing through life, spending my substance as fast as I can. The prodigal daughter with no one to welcome her home with a fatted calf. Not even any pigs.

Last night I didn't meditate before I went to bed, as I had planned to do, although there was no reason not to. I wasn't tired. I just decided to let myself off the hook. And then a similar thing happened this morning, in that I didn't get up when I first woke up, although this is one of the things I had resolved I would do in future. What is this reluctance to follow my own best advice? If I can't follow a plan when there are no constraints of worry, exhaustion, illness, time, or anything else, when *will* I do what I really want? I guess the question is: What do I really want?

What I want is for things to happen naturally without my having to arrange them. When I am sick I take the medicine the doctor prescribes but withhold my faith and then see if the medicine works on its own. Very often, of course, it doesn't. I believe that 50 percent of a cure's efficacy comes from faith, which is why placebos are often so effective. Here I am making resolutions, or at least forming guidelines, and then expecting an extra period of meditation or getting out of bed to happen spontaneously. But how is anything going to take place without my participation? I have to stay together, not be divided against myself. If I see that something needs to be done, I must move forward and do it, not hold part of myself back to see if the rest of me is going to succeed. Because the part of me that holds back is the part that has the power. If there is no separation between different parts of me, then all my strength will be in one place. In addition, there will be no commenting from the part of me that refuses to take any action.

According to the dictionary, "resolve" means not only to "make a decision" but "solve again," "intensify the solution," "cause to go back to a liquid state," "unite," "release," "separate into constituent parts," and "render visible." It has to do with a lack of settling, a looseness or fluidity, not being stuck in one place. All these meanings are suddenly released by examining one small word. This must be the answer I have been looking for. I had thought of a resolution as a peaceful end state, but now I see that it has to do with not being fixed on anything particular, with being able and willing to move in any direction.

If I really treasured these activities and the increased measure of consciousness they bring, I wouldn't avoid them so often. I would avail myself of every opportunity for freedom. It may be a human tendency to skive off on every possible occasion, but after a lifetime of the inappropriate application of effort, surely I can direct my effort to something useful?

After I'd written this, I sat down to talk to my friend Tova, who was visiting from California, about what might be going on here and what her experience is. She thought that maybe I am being too hard on myself. After such a long period of devotion to work, my pendulum is probably still swinging the other way, and the perfect balance I am looking for may come later. Also, of course, what I'm trying to do is play, so why castigate myself for not working harder at playing? Perhaps all these activities will end up as play, but as I am still on a learning curve with some of them, they definitely require a great deal of energy and attention at the moment and have not yet become play.

Lately I have been doing a little "freewriting." Just typing whatever comes into my head without censoring it. It has been interesting to see where this takes me. In this early-morning experiment I am not writing for a particular purpose, except perhaps to explore. Once thoughts have leaked out of my unconscious and found their way into words on the page, they are no longer using up energy by being locked inside me. Is this the actualization that Jung speaks of? Uniting the inner and outer consciousness makes for a free flow in whatever direction the mind moves. After I had been trying freewriting for a few weeks, I began to wonder whether, if I was able to go into every situation in the spirit of exploration, that might shift my attitude.

I have this sensation of scouring my mind, look-ing for any wisps or strands of thoughts that have been lingering in the background. Bringing them into the light of day enables me to examine and evaluate them, and choose to put them to good use or simply let them go. It is not that I am running around look-ing for them. I am just sitting here quietly waiting. There is always some movement going on in the mind, so it is unlikely that nothing fresh will surface. All the stuff I have accumulated in this lifetime is roiling around inside, rising and falling with the tide.

It is somewhat like what happens on most morn-ings, either in the bath or shower or when I am pre-paring to meditate. Odd things waft by, and I can either latch onto them or not. Once one of these thoughts has surfaced, it will hover in memory for an hour or so, revisiting me from time to time to make sure that I haven't forgotten it. I find that these reminders oc-cur in a very timely fashion, rather like little alarm clocks, and I am very grateful for them.

When I write the situation is slightly different, in that I am deliberately creating a space for the thoughts to surface rather than being surprised by them. I be-come aware of what is idling on the periphery of my vision. It is like looking around a room and estimat-ing whether it needs cleaning and, if so, in what way.

It is an active process and, as such, is probably less organic than acknowledging and welcoming thoughts that turn up when I am not summoning them from dark crevices.

All the teachings that are coming to me now are about letting go—relaxing the stomach muscles and the tension in my back and shoulders—whether it is in painting, tai chi, meditation, work, or companionship. Nothing in this is new, but never before has it seemed so clear. If I can make this major shift, who knows what might follow? Tightness in the body has to do with anticipation, with wanting a particular result, so the lesson here is to stay put, to be content with the only moment that is guaranteed: this one. Why worry about another moment that may never happen? Only this moment has been given. In this world there are no guarantees.

I have spent my life trying to ensure that nothing bad will ever happen to me and mine, and to that end I have steeled myself inside and out. This kind of insurance has been far more costly than the one I could have paid for with dollars. Yet we have to accept whatever comes our way. We have no other choice. So today I am trying a new approach: not feeling so squeezed, so in a box, which is, of course, of my own making. Welcoming everything. Not being fazed by it all. Feeling able to relinquish whatever arises in any and every given moment. I will see how deeply I can go into whatever I am doing rather than how fast or how far. It's all been the wrong dimension so far. However, "one day in Thy house" is all it takes.

At the end of 2002, Random House moved to new premises, and when I went there for the first time I had to get a new ID card. I explained to the young man taking the photos that I wasn't an employee but an independent contractor who came in every week (my imprint, Bell Tower, belongs to Random House). He asked whether that meant I was self-employed, and when I said yes, he printed out my card, and there I was with my name above my face and the word SELF in huge letters beneath it. I had been revealed at last. I felt a little like Mullah Nasruddin in one of the many Sufi stories about his antics. When he went to the bank to cash a check, he was asked for ID. When he wanted to know why, he was told that they had to be certain that he was who he said he was. So he took a mirror out of his pocket, looked at it, smiled broadly, and said to the teller, "Yes, this is me."

It was interesting to watch all my anxieties fade as the day proceeded. I had anticipated so much difficulty in finding a home for my three boxes of books and papers in the new building; not only had the boxes arrived safely but another editor offered me un-limited space on his shelves. Then, there was no line to get the new ID. Finally, the person I had to see at the book clubs was indeed there when I arrived. So all the problems melted away as I approached them, and I remembered a lovely definition someone had sent me earlier in the week: "Worrying is praying for what you don't want." I don't know who said this but she was so right.

I had been searching for a tai chi chuan teacher in the Wu style. My teacher, Sophia Delza, died some time ago, and I did not take classes from her in her final years. Almost everyone in New York City practices the Yang style, which is very different, and every at-tempt I had made to find a Wu teacher had failed until I met a long-lost acquaintance at a party and he mentioned that he himself practiced the Wu style and knew of someone who taught it. I joined the ad-vanced class the next day and the form began to come back. The movements and their sequence are all stored in my body's memory, so it is a matter of reconnect-ing to what is there, just like swimming or riding a bi-cycle. Of course, I had developed some bad habits over the years of practicing alone, or not practicing at all (more of the latter than the former, I admit). The main thing I had been omitting was the softness and gentleness that is the essence of tai chi. There is often tension in my hands and spine. Barry, my new instructor, is helping me to relinquish the hardness in my stance and allow the energy to flow through my body so that I am rooted in my feet and centered in my *tantien* in the solar plexus. This is a real boon.

I notice that my mind rebels against certain things, particularly when I try to marry the descriptions of the movements in Sophia Delza's book, *T'ai Chi Ch'uan* with the actual experience. Something in me has decided that it is very difficult, if not impossible, to follow her precise instructions and that, like map reading in a car, it won't work without another person present. I have this theory about driving in unfamiliar territory: that you need one person to drive, another to read the map, and a third to look out for road signs. This is born of a great deal of bad experience in trying to read maps and look for signs at the same time and missing the road signs as you look down at the map to double-check where you are. With tai chi, I feel as though I am trying to fulfill all three functions on my own and that my efforts are doomed to failure, so I am unwilling even to embark on the endeavor, although the step-by-step instructions are exactly what

I need. Sophia always used to say that one should practice one small part of the form at a time. How obstinate I can be when I choose to, even though it is so self-defeating.

When I was practicing recently, I noticed that each time I go over a particular form and concentrate on improving a few movements, this helps to restore the whole form. My body is gradually re-membering the fine points of the exercise. This is a great relief because I was afraid that I had forgotten whole chunks of it and would have to start from scratch. It turns out that if I start the ball rolling and keep refining the action, eventually the body memory is restored. This seems to tie in with what I have observed in the past. Repetition of a learned action eventually locks it into your system. All the time I was trying to re-member the form and making attempts to practice movements didn't quite trigger the accurate memory, but once I had got something exactly as I had been taught so many years ago, then the movement resumed its life and began to flow of its own accord. Once this takes place, it is useful to practice it a few times to strengthen and support the rekindled memory.

Each moment that you can break the iron grip of "doing" is a triumph. It's like an electrical connection. If you interrupt it, there is an immediate effect.

So I am grateful for any moment that I can step back from it all and, particularly, any moment of such release that happens spontaneously.

This lesson of letting go of all effort and tension also came to me from a brushpainting teacher who told me to allow the energy to flow of its own accord, which it will do if you don't keep limiting it and directing it where you think it ought to go.

I had gone to the Asia Society to look for a brushpainting class, which they didn't offer, but one of the places they suggested was the New York Buddhist Church. I called the church immediately and left a message. No one called back, so a couple of weeks later I called again and got the same result. It took a great deal of perseverance to connect with the instructor, Hiroshi, but eventually I was successful and arranged to attend his class the following Saturday morning.

Hiroshi met me at the door when I turned up. He was a gentle, soft-spoken soul who had been a kimono painter in his native Kyoto and was now a textile designer. The class meets in an elegant old building overlooking the Hudson River. We removed our shoes, carried a table and chairs into the beautiful upstairs shrine room, and laid newspapers over the table and the floor. There were two other students. Both women had some facility with the Japanese language, though not much.

Pigeons alighted from time to time on the outside of the window frames, and through the glass doors I could see two other small classes, one in traditional dress practicing Japanese dance, and one around a table studying dharma.

After we had ground our ink, Hiroshi came to each of us in turn and demonstrated how to write a particular Japanese character. For me he drew *kokoro*, which means "heart/mind": a medium-sized downward stroke on the left, then a fresh down-stroke that veered off to the right and up again, followed by two small down-strokes that ended with a flick of the brush, straddling the end of the big middle stroke. Hiroshi took my hand so that we could make the strokes together and then dropped it immediately. I think he was horrified at how tense I was. Too much effort as usual. He massaged my shoulders a little, and then we tried again, with slightly better results.

What Hiroshi teaches is called *unpitsu*, a word describing the movement of the body and also of the brush, an unfettered expression of the mind and spirit. He explained to me that the form and technique were not as important as allowing the free flow of energy to rise from the base of the spine. The brush is held lightly so that someone can almost take it from your fingers. I had read about this approach before but not found a teacher who insisted upon it.

I kept painting kokoro on old pages of the *New York Times* but without managing to caress the paper with the brush the way Hiroshi had described. After about three-quarters of an hour, he wrote all three characters on a sheet of good paper with one of his big brushes dripping with ink and asked each of us to write ours. The sheets were then laid out to dry on the floor.

After that, Hiroshi draped a full sheet of paper across the table, handed the brush to me, and asked me to paint a cat. I was a little taken aback, since he was giving absolutely no instruction, but I managed a rather childish image of the back of a cat with whiskers sticking out at the top and a tail swooshing around the bottom. After the cat, the three of us took turns at painting a bamboo stalk. Then he blindfolded himself with a bandana and drew a long, strong black stroke with one of his huge brushes. Talk about working from not-knowing. He grinned mischievously as he removed the kerchief from his eyes. And then, suddenly, the lesson was over.

Hiroshi would have been an ideal teacher, having the ancient tradition of the brush firmly in mind, but I hadn't known beforehand that the main focus of his class was Japanese calligraphy. Over the years I have happily studied various Roman alphabets, as well as Sanskrit and Hebrew calligraphy, because I have some familiarity with the languages that use them but it's frustrating to be drawing letters you cannot read or understand. I really didn't want to learn Japanese calligraphy, so in the end I decided not to join the class on a regular basis but take the essence of what I had received that day and incorporate it into my practice.

In the last few months I have had the sensation of floating. It is hard to tell whether this is because I am not facing any maxi or mini crisis at present. There are definitely times when I am content to sit and wait to see what turns up. I am no longer striving so hard. The spirit of inquiry perches on one of my branches, its head cocked on one side, alert and waiting. The other image that comes to mind is of the sea and its tides. The waves beat upon the shore and, day after day, odd fragments are cast up on the beach, each with its own history. Hardly anything arrives whole, and it is often a mystery as to what the original creatures and objects were and how they functioned. Yet the time they have spent in the ocean and the drubbing they have endured has stripped them of all that was superfluous, and often just the skeletons or shells remain.

When our gaze falls on such artifacts from our lives, vague memories stir within us, and if we are patient, the significance of each one may reveal itself. If not, there is always another tide twelve hours later that will discharge more flotsam and jetsam from the storehouse within.

My life appears to be "thinning out." Fewer and fewer demands are being put on me, and I am spending a great deal of time at home by myself. This is okay, as long as I accept being alone as much as being with others. I guess the crunch will come when there is "nothing" to do. Will I be comfortable and content with nothing? The truth is that each time activity appears to have died down, something new arrives on my doorstep. The key is satisfaction—being willing to live with whatever happens but also with what doesn't happen.

One of the things that is being engendered in me is a fuller trust in the universe that whatever I need will arrive. I may not always appreciate it if it is wearing a grim mask, but it is clear that whatever comes my way should be welcomed.

Present Tense

Immerse yourself in your practice at all times and in all your daily activities— walking, standing, sitting, or lying down. It is said that practice concentrated in activity is a hundred, a thousand, even a million times superior to practice done in a state of inactivity.

WILD IVY, HAKUIN, *translated by Norman Waddell*

 In the West we hold tenaciously to the view that thought is linear, that we start at A, proceed inevitably to B, and continue in that mode. Yet none of us experiences it that way. With the best will in the world, we cannot hold our minds on such a strict rein. They are always straying from the path. Do we cling to the illusion of a direct path because we believe that progress is inevitable if we don't allow ourselves to be distracted? We are such firm believers in step-by-step guides, even though none of us has man-

aged to follow instructions in the right order. At any given moment a flood of thoughts clamors for our attention. Yet I have never managed to spot what enables one thought to triumph over all the others or what makes it cede its place to another random zealot.

The older I get the more resigned I am to the fact that I do not and cannot think straight, even though I probably have more tenacity than many people I know. Even my attempt to capture these thoughts and set them down on the page was interrupted by an urge to make a note of a phone call that must be made the day after tomorrow (I succumbed to this), a vague memory that there was ironing to do (I turned my metaphorical back on this one), a notion that this might be a really good moment to paint (when I've finished writing, maybe), a knee-jerk response to a cousin who e-mailed me yet another series of bad jokes (I rushed to ask him to cease and desist, and then couldn't manage to stop myself from coping with other e-mail)—and I had been sitting in front of the computer for only five minutes. My mind is a maelstrom.

The following day I tried to observe what was going on in my mind so that I could unmask the enormous pull that happens each time I decide to devote myself completely to some activity. I spotted that after even as short a time as two minutes into whatever it is, I usually look for ways to cut out and take care of something else. Not that I abandon what I am doing forever, but I don't stick with it. My mind seeks to escape what it has told me it would like to do now. Any excuse will suffice. The message that seeped into my consciousness on that day was that the hood of the jacket I had just washed and hung in the bathroom might have slipped off the rail into the bath and so I ought to go and check up on it. Then that this would be the ideal time to make the bed or do the mending. There is no way that any of these situations could be construed as time sensitive. They were definitely distractions. I know full well that my underlying aim is to penetrate as deeply as possible into whatever is in front of me and that this is not going to happen if I keep behaving like a butterfly. What on earth is it that perpetuates such ridiculous behavior?

It is certainly not that I am incapable of long stretches of full attention. When I am occupied with something to do with my editorial work, then I slog on for hours without a second thought. My devotion is complete when it is a question of doing something for another person, but when it is for myself, it falters.

I observe myself diving into mountains of work as soon as it arrives on my coffee table rather than choosing to spend time on all the other activities I am trying to incorporate into my day. There is a relentless push to get all the work done before I can contemplate anything else. I wonder whether this has anything to do with the fact that my work provides a certain satisfaction that I am not certain I will find in other activities. After so many years, there is no possibility that I cannot tackle anything in the editorial work. I have confidence in my ability, while with the new activities that I have undertaken I know that I still have much to learn and I may not enjoy them yet as much as I would like to. All of which boils down to the fact that I am looking for results. If I can't get "it" right, then I go out of my way to avoid the undertaking. Big insight. Particularly since it is my avowed aim to take delight in each moment, to appreciate what is actually there, and not look for something else. If I am not there to observe it, I will never know how to improve my performance and become proficient in the skills that I have elected to pursue. I think I need to take another look at Madeline Bruser's book *The Art of Practicing,* which I published several years ago. The answers are all there: give precise attention, relax, enjoy, don't make any move of which you are not conscious. I remember that Madeline wrote that it was more important to be present for one note played on the piano than to spend an hour practicing automatically and not hearing any of the music.

The phenomenon arises most often when I decide to do something that I associate with a practice of attention, such as writing or painting. A tussle ensues between the part of me that has decided to commit this period of time and attention to the task and another part that seeks to deflect it to something insignificant that can easily be done later. I am determined to watch more closely and see if I can catch sight of what continually drags me away from the present. It has to be an old habit that I have been nurturing all my life and that has only come to light since I left full-time employment and have the opportunity to observe it. Once I see what it is, I will have the chance to relinquish it.

In the pursuit of a clear mind, there seem to be two possible approaches to life, and I am not yet sure which works best. The first is not to swerve from what I am doing no matter what happens, and the other is to attend to whatever comes up even if it is an interruption. Years ago an editor from San Francisco expressed his horror at the way we worked in New York publishing. He had watched as people walked into colleagues' offices and, without any compunction, interrupted whatever was going on there as though their business took precedence over everything else. He commented that he was amazed that no one who was interrupted in this way seemed bothered by it. I had never thought about this before, and I asked him how things were different in his office. He told me that he never allowed himself to be interrupted and that phone calls and other people who wanted to talk to him had to wait until he had finished whatever it was he was doing.

One Sunday recently I thought I had the whole day to myself, but as soon as I had begun to paint, the phone started to ring and didn't stop. An author wanted to tell me of the new title he had thought up for his book, and ten minutes later another wanted to make arrangements to meet that day. Then my son called and asked me to look up something for him, and a friend wanted to come and use my computer to check out her new website since her monitor's colors were inaccurate. Yes, I could have held back from answering the phone or screened my calls. Maybe I hadn't noticed that I'm available to everyone else but not to myself. I suppose it doesn't matter as long as I don't resent being interrupted, but if it is resentment that is arising, I must take steps to resolve this. Do I want to make certain activities sacrosanct? What is important is giving full attention to whatever is happening in the moment, whether it is painting or answering the phone. One activity isn't intrinsically more worthy than another in and of itself. I think that that is why I have always allowed myself to be interrupted. I believe that giving attention to others is the quickest route to "salvation" and more significant than anything I may choose to do for myself.

Perhaps my incessant shifting from one activity to another is because it is not possible for me, at least for now, to sustain a high intensity of attention for more than a brief period. It could be that I have such a short attention span that I welcome interruptions so that I have a "good" reason to flit from one occupation to another. I may have perfected this way of operating out of years of having little choice.

After I had typed these few lines, the phone rang again, and I had a chance to talk this over with a friend. She considers herself at the opposite end of the spectrum, in that when she feels that something needs her undivided attention, she lets her machine answer her phone and asks her doorman not to disturb her by ringing the bell. She has been wondering if she has gone too far, so it was fascinating for the two of us to look closely at how we each conduct our lives. Having this conversation gives both of us a fresh slant on much that we have taken for granted for too long.

I continued to think about this in the ensuing weeks and came to the conclusion that it is hard to impose order on the chaos that surrounds us, and particularly difficult to do so by trying to hold everything else in check. Doing things with an iron hand requires tremendous energy. The only plan that I have found to work is to have a sense of what you would like to do—a mental schedule, as it were—and then see what comes up. It is usually impossible to keep on a straight course since the winds keep shifting direction, but what you can do is correct your course each time you notice that you are no longer sailing in the direction you want. In order to reach your destination, you need a map, a vessel in good working order (your mind and body), and a compass or equivalent method of steering. Only then is it possible to deal with the vicissitudes that can and do arise on every journey, whether it is across the bay or into the basement to retrieve some old papers. Also, of course, you need good sea legs to enable you to keep your balance as the boat yaws beneath your feet at angles you didn't even know were possible.

Life is a rather uneasy marriage of order and chaos. If your workspace is in constant confusion, it is hard to find the tools you need for whatever you want to do, so the job is likely to get done less quickly and efficiently than it might. Some measure of order has to be introduced so as to achieve the desired result. If you happen to live, as I do, in the other camp, where the illusion of order reigns, then you have to cut yourself a little slack because nothing goes exactly like clockwork except a clock. The other thing to remember is that, in addition to your goal, you must keep your attention open at all times or you will miss vital information.

In many ways, the relationship between order and chaos is similar to that between freedom and responsibility. Both halves of the equation are necessary. We need freedom in order to be able to respond appropriately and we need to be responsible in order to use our freedom well. Order guides us through turbulence, but if there were no turbulence, life would be very straitlaced and not much fun. Disorder and chance open up many more possibilities in any and every moment.

There is so much randomness in the universe—at least from our perspective—that we rarely have enough information to allow us to get from A to B without being sidetracked. The secret is not to get upset when this happens but just take each small thing in our stride. It is part of the ongoing journey.

I have been reading *Knee Deep in Grace,* by Amy Schmidt, about the life and teaching of the diminutive Indian saint Dipa Ma. Dipa Ma's unremitting devotion to mindfulness and meditation and her wholehearted care for the welfare of everyone she met have made me ashamed of the way I have been spending my evenings—reading, watching television, or going to bed early because I can't think of anything worth staying up for. I recalled a conversation I had with another editor just before I quit my job. She was envious of me because she wished she were in a position to give herself entirely to spiritual practice. I see that although I have been working at home for several years, I have not really used the time as well as I might have. I had not wished to set myself a fixed timetable of activities. I wanted to be free to do whatever was appropriate in any given moment. But somehow I have lost sight of the whole purpose of the endeavor. It is time to get back on track and not squander any more of my life.

I have been puzzling about why particular thoughts arrive in my mind at one moment rather than another. Last night I changed purses when I went out to dinner. Half a block from home I realized that I had forgotten to bring either a pen or a pencil with me. I usually carry both but had neglected to transfer them into the smaller purse. So why did that thought arrive then, rather than earlier or later or at the moment when I needed something to write with?

I suppose the answer is as unfathomable as why meditation is difficult at some times and easy at others. I have been using a method of meditation in which you scan each area of the body minutely, proceeding from the top of the head down to the toes, including your inner organs if you can manage it (which I can't). I find that I need to dwell patiently in each area until the sensation is palpable, and this can take some time. The procedure calls for an orderly progression from top to bottom and then back again. For weeks on end I have no problem with this, and then, mayhem breaks loose, and I find that I have been sitting on my cushion for a long while without even beginning the practice, or my attention has migrated from inside my left ear to the fingertips of my right hand. I remember a book by the neurologist Richard Restak called *The Brain Has a Mind of Its Own*. Perhaps the mind is resistant to any agenda and prefers to exhibit its innate quality of freedom whenever you let it off the leash for a fraction of a second.

There is another meditation technique where you follow the mind as it leaps from one place to the next and don't attempt to restrain it in any way, but I don't find this grasshopper practice works any better than the other one. There are still huge lacunae in my attention, and it takes some time before I come to and realize which leaf or branch I have landed on. We notice a change of direction only when we wake up. The rest of time we just coast along.

In Japan, I stayed for some days at a country *ryokan,* or traditional inn. Early one morning, I visited the john. When I had finished my business, I found that there was no way to leave because there was something wrong with the door handle. It was about 5 A.M., and I couldn't hear anyone else moving about. I wiggled the lock and even tried to force it but without any luck. Then I stood on the seat and surveyed the prospects for climbing out of the window or over the door. Neither seemed a good idea. The window was tiny, no one was visible in the rice fields, and the drop from the second floor into the garden sloping away below looked quite dangerous. I was wearing nothing but my *yukata* (cotton kimono) and didn't relish jumping either with it on or off. The door to the john was a makeshift affair, and there were rough edges along the top. If I missed my footing trying to get down on the other side of the door, I might do myself a great deal of damage. It didn't seem worth the risk. So I sat down on the seat and decided to do a thorough body scan. I'd promised myself that if I were ever in captivity, I would use the time to go much deeper into this practice. This seemed to be the moment I had been waiting for, but before I could even settle my mind, I heard the sound of running water and banged on the door to attract attention. A fellow traveler who had been brushing his teeth at the sink outside the bathroom quickly came to my rescue. Apparently, his wife had been in the same position the night before, so he understood the problem.

I had one other unnerving meditation experience while in Japan. Our group had been invited to visit Tofuku-ji temple in Kyoto and have lunch with Keido Fukushima Roshi, who is the head of his lineage. We had seen a number of extraordinary temples in the previous week but nothing to rival Tofuku-ji, which is a National Treasure. The scale of the buildings and gardens and their stark opulence were almost overwhelming.

We were shown around by a competent young monk who took us to the gigantic 650-year-old zendo, which seats five hundred but is no longer used for daily practice. He asked whether we would like to sit zazen and we gladly accepted. I had just settled my body and was expecting my mind to join me soon when he picked up the *kyosaku*, sometimes known as the "encouragement stick," and stood in front of the person at the end of the row. There was a loud thwack. He took one step and paused in front of the next person, and I heard another loud thwack. The sound sent my mind spinning, and I began to wonder what I would do when he reached me. I had never been to a zendo where the kyosaku was used, but I had read about the practice. However, I had forgotten that although in the dim and distant past it was employed for waking up sleepy practitioners and acting as a startling reminder of what they were meant to be doing, it is now used only when a student invites it by making the gesture of *gassho* (a bow with the hands together) and leaning over. The monk would certainly not strike anyone unless he was asked to do so. My heart beat faster and faster as he approached, half-remembering the procedure but wondering whether he was operating by the same rules, since he had struck everyone in the line so far. He passed me by and strode jauntily toward the other side of the zendo. It was the nearest thing I have seen to a monk swaggering. This seemed most unusual for one who wields the encouragement stick. I was relieved, but I had worked myself into such a tizzy that I was hardly able to calm down before the sitting was over and we were continuing our tour of the grounds.

Whenever we look out at the world, we do so with a certain perspective. We are never in a position to see everything all at once; each take on the universe is just one point of view. But this is as it should be. This is the bounty of diversity. On the other hand, there is nothing that cannot be seen in whatever we look at, if our gaze penetrates deeply enough. Each moment is a hologram and our attention is the tool that illuminates everything going on there—or not. Emerson understood this. In his essay "Spiritual Laws," he wrote:

> The object of the man . . . is to make daylight shine through him, to suffer the law to traverse his whole being without obstruction, so that on what point soever of his doing your eye falls it shall report truly of his character, whether it be his diet, his house, his religious forms, his society, his mirth, his vote, his opposition.

I find this when I am on a train looking at the other passengers. You can appreciate a great deal about who they are just by their dress, their posture, the quality of their attention. You don't need to go and visit them in their homes, although that would reveal even more.

Attention is like a thread that hovers in the swirling

winds of the mind. When I was taking a course at the China Institute I would gather up the things I needed to take with me: brushes, ink, paints, paper, paperweight, felt mat, and paper towels. Each week I forgot a different something. So one night I decided to pack everything up methodically the night before. The next morning, I realized that I had forgotten to include sheets of paper, but as I crossed the room to retrieve the paper, my eye caught something else, and I didn't remember the paper for another ten minutes. In fact, I was lucky that I remembered it before I left the house. Here it is easy to see how little it takes to distract me. I can often look back and see what it is that has distracted me, but I still have not observed what causes a thought to resurface in my mind.

Attention is the all-important key, since the *shuen* paper on which we paint is so absorbent. A moment's hesitation with the brush, and the indelible ink or paint bleeds unevenly beyond the edges of the stroke. The intention must be clear and the concentration and movement steady. Otherwise, the effort is all for naught. What I see is that I am far from achieving even one of these elements. In class one week, the teacher, Zhan, came by and looked at my pine needles and told me to make them finer. "They are needles," he said. "Yes," I replied, "I know that, and I am trying to paint them that way but they come out thick." "All join at base," he said. "Yes," I responded, "I understand, but it doesn't come out that way." "Overlap," was his final offering. "Yes," I mumbled. "That's what I was trying to do." He was telling me nothing I did not already know about the convention of painting pine needles, but I had none of the basic principles of painting operating, so what came out on the page was pitiful. Still, I did not leave the class despondent. Eventually I said, "Maybe after the first twenty-five years, it becomes easier." He gazed at me quizzically for a moment as the import of my words percolated into Chinese, and then his face lit up with a big grin.

When I got to the last class in the semester, I chose not to copy any of Zhan's paintings and asked if he would show me some of the basic strokes so that I could spend my time practicing those and establish the groundwork. He was very willing to do this and spent some time demonstrating them for me. Then I practiced sheet after sheet but still with very little success. After an hour, Zhan came by again and asked how I was getting on. "Badly," I replied and indicated what I'd done. It turned out that on one particular stroke I had spent the entire time trying to move from thin to thick rather than vice versa, which is the way he had shown me. How could I have been so blind? I was thankful when the series of three-hour classes was over. Each Saturday was so stressful, even when I just attempted the single strokes. It was as though I was practicing being anxious and learning hardly anything about how to paint.

After that, I decided to take private lessons. I made several trips to art stores in Chinatown, I searched on the Internet, I made phone calls, I talked to anyone and everyone who might know of a good teacher, and many months later someone put me in touch with Wanxin.

Wanxin is a Chinese archeologist who worked in a museum before he came to this country. It has been hard for him to find work here because there is little demand for archeologists who don't speak English. I learned that he was also a calligrapher and painter, so I invited him and his wife, Ping, to tea to find out whether he would be willing to teach me. Ping speaks good English, but she seemed doubtful that her husband would be able to manage. I said that I would help him with his English if he would help me with my painting and that it was surely worth a try. "Okay," she said, "and if it doesn't work out, we can still be friends." She gave me her number at the United Nations library where she works and said that we could call her any time during the lesson if we couldn't make ourselves understood.

As it turned out, Wanxin and I have had a splendid time together for the last year, and we call Ping only when the lesson is over if it is necessary to clarify a few points. Each week he prepares something for me to copy and then guides me step-by-step through the process. He demonstrates how to do the strokes and he sits beside me like a hawk, encouraging me when things go well and stopping me immediately when I stray from the path. Having his constant and undivided attention makes all the difference to the learning process. I have lost my fear of not getting everything right, we enjoy each other tremendously, and I am having GREAT FUN.

For my part, I write down new words for him as they crop up in our conversation, and he looks them up in his little electronic dictionary and writes the Chinese beside my scrawl. Then I drill him in the correct pronunciation of each word. He goes to a class to learn English twice a week but, this being New York City, his instructor is Russian, and what he is learning there leaves a lot to the imagination.

Soon after our lessons began, Wanxin showed me how to paint trees, but my trees never look like either his trees or any real tree. One week he brought with him a small branch, so I no longer had any excuse about not knowing what a tree looks like. But even when I sat down to reproduce it on the page, I noticed my attention sloping off before I could catch it, in an effort to finish the painting. This is extremely self-defeating behavior, and I don't understand why I persist in it. What is this great reluctance to see what is in front of me? Whenever I sit down to paint something, first I study it; then I launch myself off from a particular point; look at it once more; and then focus on what I am producing on the page; and don't wake up until what I have done no longer bears much resemblance to the original.

Sometimes I tell myself sternly that I am going to make a concerted effort not to behave the way I have been doing in the past, but I still find myself commenting, "Well, that part is not very significant. I can manage that on my own. No need to copy what's there slavishly." Of course, all this wouldn't matter if I really knew what a tree or anything else looks like, but I don't.

One day after class at the China Institute I had coffee with one of the other students. He too was a relative beginner but had great talent. In talking with him, I realized that you do have to have a clear picture of what you are going to put on the paper. Otherwise, what arrives there is completely arbitrary. It may very well look good, but the shape, color, and proportion are all a matter of chance. What I do much of the time is just blunder on in the hope that I will naturally fall into the right way of doing it, as though one day I will make a stroke correctly almost by accident and ever after remember how to do it. It is amazing how often and for how long we delude ourselves. This method has never worked in the past, and there is no reason to believe that it might work in the future. Even though I tell myself that I am going to do this or that, when the moment comes, time after time I let the brush take off on its own in the hope that it will know where to go. And it doesn't. The one-pointedness I seek is right there at the tip of the brush, but where am I? I am unable to stay with the action that is taking place in that moment, watching what happens as it happens. I am always measuring it against some hypothetical bar that is raised ever higher as I approach it.

As it turns out, the best thing is a combination of all this. The other day Wanxin watched me trying to improve on a bamboo stalk I had already painted and then explained that in Chinese painting, if what comes out on the page differs from what is in your head, you just leave it as it is. You can always try again, but you can't change the past. Don't think of it as a mistake. It is what it is and may very well be a realistic bamboo even if it is different from your idea of bamboo.

Now I have at last perceived what is going on, and the task at hand is to use this knowledge to move forward and take a fresh approach to these new skills. Every time I notice a black hole in my attention—for instance, I perform a movement in the tai chi form and come to the end of it without knowing how I got there—I need to go back and repeat the movement and be present to it. Otherwise I am just practicing inattention, and whatever you practice, you become very good at.

It is not a question of practicing for a certain amount of time or painting a certain number of pages. It is what happens in each moment of practice that counts. I mentioned earlier that the world manages to operate on automatic almost all the time. The interesting question is: How different would the world be if we were conscious of our actions?

It was bitterly cold here for weeks last spring, with no walking weather. One day the temperature rose above freezing, and the last of the ice and snow began to vanish. As I entered Riverside Park two gray squirrels scampered toward me. I stopped and said good morning to them. They dashed up a tree and ran along the branch in an effort to get close to me. I eventually got them to understand that I had nothing to offer them but goodwill. I had forgotten how intense the gaze of an animal can be. It bore right into me and anchored me in place, and twenty minutes later I was still enlivened by it. It gave me the precision and focus I needed to enter the day. Before I engaged with the squirrels my morning had been more than a little blurred.

Our ability to think and dream is certainly a gift, but more often than not it draws us inward, and we lose our connection to what is actually happening in the outside world. There has to be a way to embrace these two views so that we are not lost to what is going on but are able to use whatever is available in the present moment to move forward into the next. You never see a squirrel with a hazy look in its eyes. It is either awake or asleep, and its dreams are reserved for the time it spends with its eyes shut.

Considering all the traffic problems I encountered the next day, I am amazed how calm I stayed as, because of street closures, the buses carried me several miles out my way in order to get across Central Park. In the past I would have been beside myself with resentment, but now it didn't seem so important. Without realizing it I may have been still under the spell of those squirrels, gazing out at the world without a fixed idea of what should or should not be happening, just being interested in all that was going on around me. Opening out, opening out.

I used to believe that monks and nuns were in an enviable position because they were off in monasteries devoting themselves full-time to contemplation of the Divine. I fantasized that everything must be much easier in such an environment. But, of course, even if you live apart from the hurly-burly of the modern world, your mind is always there with you. It may be slightly easier to catch sight of our mental shenanigans when we are not distracted by earning a living, accommodating and caring for family members, and withstanding the onslaught of the media, but it is no easier to deal with the squirming of our minds. I say all this because many people may think that because I am doing freelance work and my son has left home, I am now living in an ideal environment. Being on your own certainly has its advantages, but like life in a monastery, it doesn't remove the basic problem of how to keep track of your mind and persuade it to follow your instructions. Would it were that simple.

Coming Unstuck

Nothing whatsoever is to be clung to
as me or mine.

THE BUDDHA

Shunryu Suzuki Roshi, the author
of the classic *Zen Mind, Beginner's
Mind*, clarified what the Buddha said
when he taught that zazen is the
state of mind in which you do not stick to anything.

We do our best to cling to every kind of object
and idea, as though our very identity depended on
such attachments. Why do certain things get fixed in
our minds so firmly, even though they are untrue?
This is something I often do with quotations and
stories—things that I think I know without a doubt
but that prove to be untrue when I check them carefully. Recently it also happened with the address of a
place I was about to visit. I was convinced that it was

on Fifty-third or Fifty-fourth Street even though the invitation specified Fifty-ninth. What this has shown me is that I cannot rely on any facts that are in my brain. It turns out that most, if not all, the information there is slightly tainted. What I have stored there might be true but probably isn't, and even if it is "accurate," all of it is being seen only from my limited point of view. Even scientific facts often turn out to be untrue decades or centuries later. I suppose all one can do is greet every fact with a welcoming smile or a sardonic grin and let it sit there. Never put too much weight on such thin ice.

I become very discombobulated when I am pulled away from the norm. I try to avoid hassles, streamlining my life so that everything runs smoothly along straight and familiar tracks. I don't like it when I am forced to spend more time, money, or energy on something than I think it requires. But sometimes circumstances put me (just like everyone else) in such situations. Each time I try to arrange things to make my life easier, I am ensuring that I don't learn anything. I tend to react as though the universe is just trying to make life difficult for me, while the truth is that life is hard for everyone. Some people simply deal with this, and some grouse and kick against the pricks. I am one of the latter. I forget that it is the hard times that teach us something and give us a chance to grow. Not that we should seek out adversity—but we should accept it. It may be going too far to say that we should be grateful for it, but at least we should stop trying to refuse the situation. I have brought myself to the point where I can be open to what arrives in my schedule, but I am still hoping that whatever it is will be pleasant and meaningful, rather than just whatever it is.

We not only try to stick grimly to what we think we know but we also hold firmly to what we don't know—one way of perpetuating our ignorance and keeping ourselves in the dark. I have been practicing yoga on my own for more than forty years, having started by studying a book I discovered in the library where I worked at my first job, and very occasionally since then going to a weekend or single class of instruction. Last year I joined a weekly class for the first time, and it was a fascinating experience. Almost everything that Jill, the instructor, taught was in Silva, Mira, and Shyam Mehta's *Yoga: The Iyengar Way*, which I had published twelve years earlier—yet I had never focused on it. So much is below our radar screens.

We discard a great deal of the information that is available to us. It is not possible to store everything in our brains, so we are always being selective, but it is strange that we reject (that is, don't select) so much that would be really useful to us. I have never bothered with most of the names (either in Sanskrit or English) of the poses in yoga or the different positions in tai chi, so when a teacher or student mentions them, I usually draw a blank. Yet it would be useful to know the terminology so that I could relate to what others are talking about.

Because I have always practiced on my own, I have little sense of which part of my body is which. I mean that I don't label it. So when I started the yoga class and Jill said, "Stretch your right leg back," I couldn't do it immediately. I have never been able to identify my right and left sides without thinking about it, so when I hear "right leg," I have to work out which is the right side and then send an instruction to my leg. By that time, there have been several more instructions and I have missed them. I didn't experience this problem if I watched what Jill was doing and reversed it in my mind to compensate for the fact that she was facing the class, even though this is a much more complicated procedure. I am embarrassed to admit that when I was a child and had difficulty distinguishing between left and right (also east and west), I would superimpose a map of the British Isles over whatever it was. I knew that Wales was to the west of

England (both *Wales* and *west* began with *W*, which was a great help). The way maps are drawn, Wales was always on the left of the page. Once I had got this mental map firmly in place, I could then figure out which side or direction was west or east. Unfortunately, this is often what happens even today.

One of the things I liked about Jill's class was that it strengthened my meditation (and every other kind of) practice as it explored the emotional and physical spaces in the body and illuminated how these are really the same thing. She taught what she described as spaciousness and openheartedness. It is not that I hadn't been aware of this, but it is wonderful to find someone who will work with you on releasing the things in your body or your life that are either tight or blocked. She identified much inside me that I had been ignoring for decades. If you are not aware of something, you never attempt to do anything about it. You don't even have the choice.

For instance, I told her that I have a problem with my right hip: it dislocates from time to time because I have very shallow hip sockets. She observed that I favor that hip and list to the left when I am standing. This makes sense when you think about it, but it has been so subtle and so ongoing that I have never spotted it on my own. No wonder I have had such difficulties in both tai chi and yoga keeping my balance when I try to stand on one foot.

Without reaching out—in this case by signing up for a yoga class at last—we are often unlikely to find out many things we need to know. I have definitely become too isolated in my thinking, believing that I know what is best for my body and my psyche, when, in reality, I am just overlooking vital aspects of my life that need reconstitution.

As I mentioned earlier, we are—I am—forever trying to arrange our lives to make them conform to how we would like them to be, to organize everything for our ultimate comfort and satisfaction. After I had been happily attending the yoga class for five months I found, to my horror, that it would soon be coming to an end and would not start up again in the fall because there hadn't been enough students to make a lunchtime class financially viable. This was a real blow.

It is small things like this that bring us (ruefully) back into the present and remind us that we need to treat each experience as an occasion never to be repeated. I had envisioned going to the Thursday lunchtime class year after year, systematically learning from Jill how the body functions and how to become more aware of it. If I didn't quite grasp something, there would always be another opportunity in the future. I had been coasting along on that assumption, not making the best use of my time with her. When I realized how mistaken I had been, my house of cards began to tremble.

What this showed me was that when things are going well we go to sleep a little. We smile and congratulate ourselves on the fact that nothing is going to disturb our equilibrium. Then, out of nowhere it seems, the landscape shifts, and we wake up in alarm and look around. Of course, losing a convenient time for a yoga class is not a trauma in and of itself. As it turns out, a small jolt like this is something to welcome. It is a reminder to pay close attention to this moment, and this one, and this one.

It is fascinating to see how one thing leads to another. If a friend hadn't called me on an errand of mercy recently, asking me to swell the numbers at the cabaret performance of a friend of hers, I would not have gone to my bedroom closet to change my clothes. While I was standing there, choosing something to wear, I detected a strange smell but could see nothing wrong. I got a stool from the kitchen, peered above the rack of clothes, and saw that the whole of the back wall was wet and the paint bubbling. The sound of water dripping steadily behind the wall was more than disturbing. I removed all the clothes from the closet before they were spoiled, as they had been ten years ago when this had last happened, telephoned the upstairs tenants, and left a message for the superintendent.

So often a movement in an unanticipated direction will reveal something you would never have seen if you just kept to your routine. It widens your view in unimaginable ways (including becoming aware of leaks).

One day I had lunch with Jill after the class, and it turned out that she was planning to try to persuade me to go on a week's retreat with her teacher, Tsoknyi Rinpoche. I knew about the retreat but hadn't seriously considered it, even though it is true that I have more respect for him than any other teacher I have met in my life and I had nothing to prevent me from devoting that time to being in his presence. So why say no when you can say yes?

This way of living my life is akin to what the Zen teacher Bernie Glassman calls "aimless meandering." In his book *Bearing Witness*, he describes what he and his students do when they go on "street retreats," where keeping to a schedule almost never works.

We all meander aimlessly, looking at everything from street level. We notice things we don't usually have time to notice . . . no watches on our wrists, no appointment to keep, walking everywhere but arriving nowhere. . . . We are opening up, letting go of our usual concepts. . . . The more we empty ourselves, the fuller our lives become. The irony is that most people acquire more and more things, trying to realize that fullness, only to discover instead how empty their lives are!

When you strike up a friendship with someone late in your life, there is a tremendous hurdle to overcome. Often you feel as though you have to fill the other person in on decades of history or he or she will not understand "who you are," and there is a mad gallop that takes place before you both calm down and realize that this recap is not really necessary. Yes, it is nice to know that you share so much experience and so many interests, but the only real connection is in the moment, so why not remain there and see what happens? Recently I went to lunch with a woman I met through gardening in Riverside Park. Everything about the visit was lovely except for this attempt to bring each other up-to-date. Neither of us was able to hold back on the torrent of words, and we often spoke at the same time. I doubt that either of us will remember most of what was said because of this. The next day I took the unusual step of pointing this out when I thanked her for her hospitality. I thought that if both of us were aware of how ridiculous the urge was, we could dispense with it and just be comfortable with each other now, without bringing "then" into the relationship at all.

The fact that we were having lunch at all is remarkable. One evening in the fall the Riverside Park Fund gave a "thank you" dinner for all its volunteers at the open-air rotunda by the Seventy-ninth Street Boat Basin. Although dusk was falling, I decided to walk there through the park, even though I don't normally venture into the park on my own after the light fails. I was gazing at the corkscrewed moonflower buds in the community garden and hoping that one of them might spring open while I stood there, when a slim and very upright woman strode past. Something about her bearing and determination made me think that she was probably on her way to the dinner, and I set off at a clip so that I could draw level with her and ask if she was going to the same place as I was. It turned out that I had guessed correctly. We walked along the promenade together but went our separate ways once we arrived at our destination. Although, as it turned out, we lived only three blocks from one another, our paths had not crossed before, and indeed the only times we ran into one another over the next few months was in the park. It seems that I have the moonflowers and my impetuosity to thank for this new friendship.

Then a manuscript by Cynthia Bourgeault arrived in the mail. Cynthia is an author I once edited, and she had asked me to provide a "blurb" for the cover of her new book *The Wisdom Way of Knowing.* When I began to read her manuscript, I was struck that she had been dwelling on many of the same questions I had in relation to attention and surrender. Not that she was telling me a great deal that I wasn't aware of already, but she managed to make so many connections between different facets of knowledge that the whole subject was suddenly lit up and became accessible and practical.

As I read what she had to say about our role in Creation being to see what is actually going on, that the Divine creates but needs someone to acknowledge the manifestation to complete the act, everything became very clear. This is intimately connected to one of the principles of quantum mechanics: the presence of an observer has an effect on and changes the result of the experiment. It seems to me that if I truly see what is going on—anywhere, at any time—if I am just present and my observation penetrates to the essence of the activity, then I too become part of the equation. This is my role and is why witnessing is so vital. First one sees and then acknowledgment takes place a split second later. At which point the extraneous matter becomes transparent, and I become aware of the strands that join one thing to another. We know that nothing is really separate from anything else but generally do not see the essential connections between one thing and another.

When I joined the class at the China Institute, it became clear the first week that nothing gets handed to you on a plate. I am always hoping to find an instructor who will teach me in the way I think is best. For a start the class had too many students in it—twelve—and so Zhan had little time for each of us. His English was extremely limited. One day he observed what I had done and said, "Leaves wide." I looked puzzled, and he smiled and said no more, and so I had to ask whether he meant that my leaves were too wide or not wide enough. He expected each student to choose one of his paintings, which were protected by plastic sleeves, and trace everything onto the paper before starting to paint. This meant that everyone was doing something different and there could be no general instruction. If I had been the teacher, which, of course, I was not, I would have demonstrated for part of the class so that students would be able to benefit from this if they wanted to, and everyone would attempt to paint the same thing. Many years earlier, I had taken a class from Zhan's father, Zhang Shou-Cheng. He would paint a little and then we would copy what he had done; he would come around to correct our work; then he would demonstrate the next stage; and so on. This was an extremely effective teaching method because he built up the picture in small increments.

I have listed all the negatives of the class, but of course there were also positive things to embrace. There always are. I did manage to take away several useful tips. I watched each time Zhan demonstrated something. He painted on a piece of paper towel, and I saw that if you execute the strokes correctly, there is no need to be so fussy about the quality of the paper. In order to paint well on a paper towel, you have to move fast and not waver, two things that every teacher emphasizes. The intent must be clear and bold, or the paper will absorb a huge amount of paint or ink. He used the tip of the brush most of the time, even though it was a big brush and took far more paint onto it than I had been accustomed to. I seem to add so much water to my pigments that watermarks appear on the paper after the paint has dried.

The second painting I tried was of bamboo, and when he stopped by my chair to demonstrate this, I watched him flick the brush off to the left as he finished a segment of the stalk. This was easy to emulate when it was my turn and something I was grateful to learn.

Perhaps I am too greedy. When I go to a yoga or tai chi class, so many new things are offered that I have an urge to grasp all of them and internalize them then and there. I have managed to relinquish the desire to grasp but not the regret I feel, in that I have the sense that what is being offered to me will be wasted if I do not receive all of it—as though there is a plate of delicious cookies and if I take only one, the rest will be thrown away. In any lesson, I receive only a small fraction of what I am offered. It could be that some things I am unable to welcome fully the first time will become mine when (and if) they are offered again. When I catch sight of them a second time, the earlier memory may help to transfer the relevant information into my psyche. That is all I can hope for. Each person can digest only so much in any moment, and the teacher cannot know each student's capacity, or which of the many things offered will actually be received.

Two of my classes offered far more than I could

take home, while the other appeared to offer very little. Yet from each I returned home with one, two, or perhaps three small pointers. This is probably all I am able to absorb, no matter how much is offered. I learned the same amount from each teacher, even though it appeared that two of them were being generous and one stingy. No matter what the painting teacher offered me, at that stage I was not yet able to make any more of it my own. However wonderful my teacher is, I cannot learn more than I am able and willing to receive.

The other evening an elderly woman who lives across the street came to supper. She brought a bag of small gifts and spread them out on my coffee table, urging me to choose two, which I did. She then scooped up the rest and put them back in her bag. As she did so, she picked up a slate coaster and offered it to me, "Why don't you take this too?" she said. I laughed nervously and replied, "That coaster is mine already." So she picked up another and said, "What about this one? Would you like this instead?" I told her gently that the second coaster was part of the same set.

I see a connection between this and the classes I attend. This woman, whose short-term memory is beginning to fail her, generously offered me a choice of all the useful and beautiful things she had brought with her, but she didn't expect me to take all of them. Then she offered me something I believed I already owned, and this made me appreciate it all the more. I had had these coasters for many years and hadn't been aware of them much, so in a sense she was able to make a gift of them to me. Other people are always offering us more than we are willing and able to receive. In addition, they often help us to appreciate those things that we already have in our possession.

All the hiccups in our lives loom so large and appear so calamitous because we hold them in front of our faces and obscure everything else. At such times we are rarely aware of the world around us and therefore nothing is seen in perspective. Whatever is causing us distress balloons out of all proportion. When I awoke one day recently, all my muscles and tendons were shrieking in response to the yoga stretches they had attempted the previous day. I could hardly move and ended up abandoning my early morning exercise routine and a foggy stint on my meditation cushion. I did no writing all day. My whole system closed down, and I felt cut off from the world. You would think that I had been put through an extreme form of torture rather than a belated attempt to correct my posture. We tend to focus on disruptions to the status quo and screen out everything else. We give ourselves entirely to the problem at hand and come to believe that the consequences will be dire. Then something happens to relieve the pressure, and the difficulty is no longer insurmountable; in fact, it vanishes from our consciousness for the time being.

This is what happened to me. I was completely identified with the pain in my body and not even enjoying the white, flurrying world of the snowstorm outside the window a foot or so from where I was sitting, when I received an e-mail from a friend in Tennessee announcing that she had recommended me for a fascinating and probably lucrative freelance job here in New York City. I hadn't heard from this woman for almost a year, and I was touched by her confidence in me. Whether I would eventually be hired to do the work or not, this news was enough to reconnect me to the world and all its possibilities. I stopped wallowing in my physical misery and forgot about my aches and pains for the rest of the day. This insight isn't original, of course, but it has taken me many moons to acknowledge it. I came across it thirty years ago in two quotations from the teaching of Rabbi Nachman of Bratslav, who had made these observations two hundred years ago.

All distress that man experiences comes out of himself, for the light of God is always flooded about him, but man—by stressing the life of the body too much—fashions a shadow, so that the light of God cannot reach him.

And:

Just as the hand, held before the eye, can hide the tallest mountain, so this small earthly life keeps our gaze from the vast radiance and the secrets that fill the world. And he who can draw it from his eyes, as one draws away the hand, will see the great light at the core of the world.

For a period of some months I prefaced my early morning scriptural reading with the recitation of Psalms 23 and 121. This was prompted by the fact that my sister-in-law, Valery, when she attended my mother as she was dying, accompanied her passage into the beyond with the comforting and time-honored words of the Twenty-third Psalm. When Valery told me this, I realized that had I been at my mother's bedside I would not have been able to summon up the words, so I decided that I would make sure that I had them safely in my brain in case I was ever in that situation myself. So, each morning, I spoke them aloud, and from time to time pondered their deeper meaning. Then, one day, the message of the opening line of the Psalm 121, "I will lift up mine eyes unto the hills from whence cometh my help," became clear. Whenever we lift our gaze from whatever it is that preoccupies us, then we have a chance to see the Divine working in the world.

Watch This Space

Let your hook always be cast; in the
stream where you least expect it,
there will be a fish.

THE ART OF LOVE, Ovid

 The reason I joined a group traveling
to Japan in 2003 was to immerse my-
self in Rinzai Zen by visiting some of
the rural temples where Hakuin taught
in the eighteenth century and by studying Hakuin's
painting and calligraphy. Hakuin revitalized Rinzai
Zen when it was at a low ebb. For those unfamiliar
with the two major schools of Zen, Soto and Rinzai,
I would say that the principal practice of Soto Zen is
shikantaza, "just sitting," and that of Rinzai Zen is
koans, the traditional conundrums designed to make
the mind balk. Soto temples were usually to be found
in the country, while the Rinzai school was supported by the warrior class and the imperial family in

Kyoto and is associated with calligraphy, painting, architecture, landscape, tea ceremony, painting, and Noh drama.

Once I had signed up for the trip, I thought I should do a little homework. I got hold of Norman Waddell's book *Wild Ivy*, a translation of Hakuin's autobiography with an extensive essay by the translator that sets the story in context. I learned that Hakuin had become a novice monk at fourteen, in 1699, having been terrified at the prospect of suffering in hell for sins he would undoubtedly commit during his lifetime. Even as a young boy he dedicated himself to studying the scriptures and living by them in order to avoid damnation. Over the years he searched for an authentic teacher, traveling from one temple to another (seventeen, by my count) and coming to the conclusion that almost none of the abbots he encountered understood the true nature of the Buddha's teaching. After practicing severely (there's no other word for it), he did experience realization on several occasions and eventually returned as abbot to Shoin-ji, the small country temple where he had begun his monastic life. There he taught for over fifty years until his death in 1769.

Hakuin lived in the feudal Edo period and claimed to have been born "at the hour of the ox, the day of the ox, in the month of the ox, and the year of the ox." He was strict, outspoken, and sometimes shocking—not one to suffer fools gladly. Perhaps his greatest claim to fame is the koan "Listen to the sound of one hand." No, he didn't add the word "clapping" at the end of the sentence. That got tagged on by some translator and is not there in the original. Hakuin is renowned not only as the man who was responsible for revitalizing Rinzai Zen but also as a brilliant painter, calligrapher, writer, and teacher. He did not come into his own as a painter until he was in his forties, but from that time on his paintings and calligraphy went from strength to strength, even in the last year of his life. Hakuin's aim, once he himself had achieved realization, was to help everyone, regardless of their station in life, "penetrate the great matter." To this end he used humor, slang, and caricatures. His strokes are bold, exuberant, unmitigated, without doubt. They come from a concentrated mind.

One morning while I was in Japan I tried using a fountain brush to draw the miniature tiger lilies in my room, and although some essence of tiger lily appeared on the page, the strokes were infirm, tentative, and uncertain. It was clear that I needed to abandon the doubt that is always skulking just out of view: my doubt about whether I have mastered the technique, whether it is possible for me to represent on paper what is right in front of me. I saw that it is the desire to know—to understand how the flower grows and to find a way to express that on the paper—that produces wobbly lines. The secret is just to move the brush and watch what happens *as* it happens. Observe the energy moving. Holding on to an idea of where you want to go puts a strain on the way in which you move, and the strokes you make while under the influence of this idea come in little lurches.

Of course, this is true for everything else in life too. If you have a fixed idea of the result you want, there is a fight going on at every turn. Somehow you have to have a general view of the direction you would like to take but not be so strict with yourself that the rigidity and tension affect the traveling conditions of your journey. This is tricky because if you don't have anything particular in mind to begin with, you are unlikely to make any move at all.

One of the places my companions and I visited was Ryutaku-ji ("Dragon Swamp"), the magnificent eighteenth-century Rinzai Zen temple just north of Mishima. We climbed up the steps through the tall pine trees, ferns, and bamboo to the stately monastery buildings of dark wood with their gray, bamboo-fluted, tiled pagoda roofs. We were welcomed by a monk and ushered along tatami-covered corridors with shoji screens on every side into the Great Compassion Hall, where we sat cross-legged on the floor facing Hakuin's fierce portrait of Bodhidharma, with his hooked nose, bushy beard, and furrowed brow (to me he looked like a chasidic rebbe). While Bodhidharma's enormous eyes watched us, we waited for the arrival of the diminutive Kyudo Nakagawa Roshi, who is described so endearingly in Lawrence Shainberg's book *Ambivalent Zen*.

Kyudo Roshi entered the room unobtrusively, joking in English (he spent many years in the United States) and telling us to make ourselves comfortable. This irrepressible little man is now seventy-six years old, and he sat there with his big glasses and big ears, stabbing the air with his fan to emphasize the points he was making.

"I have nothing to teach," he began. "You have to find out for yourself. I not very intelligent. In morning I wash my face. If I want to go to the toilet, I shit. Only man can think. Don't separate head from body. It is one whole body. You see by your eye. You think with the whole body. You complicate things with your head. Everything is very simple and very quiet. I can't help. You can discover what is truth through

131

your own experience. My teaching is: aimless aim, formless form. Thank you very much. I am sorry." Having thoroughly concentrated our minds, he encouraged us to explore the temple and grounds on our own, then he rose from his cushion, eyes twinkling, and left the room.

On most mornings we "sat" together before breakfast. Many people in the group belonged to the Hoen-ji Zen center in Syracuse, New York, and were used to a particular form of practice, which included chanting. The only kind of chant I really like is Gregorian chant, but this was Japanese chanting followed by an English translation, recited as though it were still in Japanese. One morning, after struggling for several days over whether to join in, I listened to the sound of the words and just let it flow over me. No participation but also no resistance, even to the bells, clappers, and incense. When we began zazen, I watched the thoughts float through my mind and heard the rain cascading down like a rushing river, the occasional cry of a bird, and the croaking of the frogs. Then I became aware of the smells from the kitchen on the other side of the screen door—first rice, then fish, and then other foods I didn't make an effort to identify. My eyes rested on the diagonal pattern of the thin green-and-yellow binding at the edge of the tatami and the nubbly sensation of the rice hulls in the pillow beneath my buttocks. My breath rose and fell, and for once there was no pull in any particular direction. Afterward the Heart Sutra was recited in Japanese, and Kaz Tanahashi produced a laptop from behind his back (digital dharma?) and read us his beautiful rendering of this sutra, in which he translated "emptiness" as "boundlessness." For the first time, I felt a possibility of understanding what is generally translated as "Form is emptiness; emptiness is form."

"Aimless aim; formless form." And: "Form is boundless." Were these saying the same thing? Is it a matter of holding both aim and aimlessness in mind at the same time? Remaining aware of the form but not feeling bound by it? Like the glass that is both half empty and half full; it has equal measure of liquid and air. Both views must be taken into account for a true understanding of the situation.

In Japan, form is of the utmost importance, and nowhere is this as evident as in temple gardens. The gardens at Ryutaku-ji offered us our first chance to appreciate the Japanese approach to nature. In front of the main building expanses of chipped stone, individual boulders, and miniaturized trees had been marshaled to suggest harmony, beauty, and stability. Each element had been arranged or was growing in its appointed place without any sign of natural chaos. The effect was tranquil but not joyous. Everything was composed, determined, limited. Was this an invitation to remain in the present, a bid to thwart our constant desire to move on to something else, or an attempt to restrict the freedom of the observer? There wasn't a tree in the garden that hadn't been trained, pruned, or manipulated in some way. And when trees were injured or grew old and frail, every effort was made to support them and encourage them to go on living: Wooden or bamboo supports were lashed together to cradle their trunks and branches. The Japanese had taken life extension to a new level. Even the trees were not allowed to fade away gracefully.

I found this lack of spontaneity both peaceful and troubling. Was it that I wasn't used to so much harmony or that I sensed that in this effort to embody perfection something vital had been confined?

The Japanese grow few flowers in their gardens. They concentrate on combining trees, mosses, plants, and ferns, in a variety of shapes, heights, densities, and colors, against a background (or foreground) of rocks, small stones, and running water. Also taken into consideration are light and shade and the angle of the trees and their girth. The only flowers visible in this and many other gardens were the salmon-colored azaleas (also camellias, but these were not yet in bloom), which were neatly trimmed into hedges. Hedges? Who in the West would dream of using azaleas for hedges? The message seemed to be: "There's no need to worry: everything is under control."

The next day we took the bullet train into Tokyo. The original plan had been to visit the two museums that had collections of Hakuin's work—the Eisei Bunko and the Idemitsu. It turned out that the former was closed for some reason, and when we reached the latter, a small museum housed on the ninth floor of a tall modern building near the Imperial Palace, we discovered that there were a couple of other exhibits on show and not one painting or piece of calligraphy by Hakuin, even though the Idemitsu owns the largest collection of Hakuin's work in the world and most of the really famous paintings. This was a great disappointment.

After a brief tour of what *was* on display, I stood at the sales counter waiting for everyone else to congregate while I leafed idly through catalogs of an artist's preliminary sketches for his porcelain designs. My attention was caught by a drawing with just a couple of petals and a single leaf visible at the edge of the paper. It would never have occurred to me to paint a blossom that was almost out of view, and my heart gave a great leap. I saw in that moment that there were countless ways of seeing things differently from the way I usually do. In the West, we tend to place the subject in the middle of the page with plenty of space around it, aiming for some measure of balance. It wouldn't occur to us not to paint the whole flower. We search for a way to get it all into the picture, even if this means making everything smaller so that it will fit.

The eighteenth-century Japanese painter Ike Taiga was once asked, "What is the most difficult thing to paint?" He replied: "The part that is not painted."

By dint of exquisite placement and juxtaposition, in traditional Japanese arts our attention is arrested time and again and we are presented with an opportunity to contemplate and appreciate discrete moments of eternity. The Japanese have refined everything to its essential elements. Theirs is a culture of illumination, highlighting instants of clarity by focusing on small details. Each movement or object is exactly prescribed, and nothing is left to chance. Spontaneity is allowed to arise but only within a certain form. Each stroke of the brush, movement of the fan, and so on stands alone as a gesture that can never be precisely replicated. There is also a strong element of modesty in everything the Japanese do, while the American way is profligate, a way of excess. Americans are always seeking more of everything, while the Japanese demonstrate how little is actually necessary. What we have is an in-your-face culture. We shout rather than whisper, while in Japan things tend to be implied rather than spelled out.

While I was in Japan, I sensed a subtle shift in my perspective that is best expressed by Roland Barthes, who observed when he was there that "every object . . . seems framed . . . yet this frame is invisible. . . . The thing is not outlined [or] illuminated, there is: *nothing,* an empty space." What I brought home with me when the visit was over was "nothing" but this space. Yet I found it hard to incorporate this emptiness into my life. To begin with I sat down to paint and, out of habit, my brush started out near the center of the page. I was halfway through the painting before I remembered that my intention had been to start out by holding the space in mind and see how to use that to balance the few blossoms I wanted to entrust to the paper. Ike Taiga had put his finger on the difficulty.

Then one day I brought home a spray of tiny pink tea roses from the garden and tried again. When I had three small flowers and a few leaves peeking out from the edge of the paper, I stopped and admired the wide open space. As I often do when I am happy with a painting, I scanned it into my computer and e-mailed it to a friend. She had just read my account of the trip to Japan and was aware of what I was aiming to do. Yet she wrote right back describing how she had fiddled with the corners of the painting on her screen for some time, doing her best to enlarge it so that she could see "the rest of the flowers" before she woke up to the fact that there were no more flowers to see. This is a perfect illustration of the different expectations in Eastern and Western art.

Even more telling is that my scanner refuses to scan empty space. When I place one of my paintings on the scanner bed, a little sign appears telling me that it is going to "optimize the image." Then it excludes the wide open space and places the flower smack in the middle of the page, where I didn't want it. I've tried and tried to remedy this but have concluded that this is the way this scanner has been trained to perform.

I thought back to when I was studying Sanskrit grammar and how I had been fascinated by the word *visheshana*, which can mean either an "adjective" or an "adverb." *Vi* is a movement out, as in distributing or broadcasting something. *Shesh* is what is left, "the remainder." So *visheshana* means "the act of distinguishing, defining, qualifying, and discriminating." *Vishesh* is that which stands out: it eliminates that which is not essential so that you can see what *is*. It uses space to draw attention to the essential qualities of something. It asks that you keep in mind what isn't there. It reminds you that the invisible is as important as the visible.

For years I thought of *visheshana* as calling out a particular attribute that was not apparent beforehand. For instance, one evening, as I came into my building the doorman asked me if I was all right. He said that I looked exhausted. Until that moment I had not realized that I was tired, but his words caused me to acknowledge my weariness and take a nap to remedy the situation. Many other adjectives could have been applied to me in that moment, but he identified that I was tired. It works the same way when you see something and realize that it is beautiful or, perhaps, ugly. What is generally forgotten at that moment are all the other qualities of whatever it is you are looking at. Once an adjective has been applied to an object, we forget everything else about it. Yet what is being singled out and emphasized is balanced and reinforced, almost supported, by what is *not* there— the unseen remainder. The other qualities are in abeyance. What the mind does naturally is focus on one thing in the same way that the lens of a camera works. You cannot focus on everything at once, either through a lens or in real life, but the evidence of things unseen must never be forgotten.

It is also instructive to look at this in relation to time. As I mentioned, I happen to be someone who always arrives everywhere early, and I am never sure how to handle the fact other people are rarely on time for appointments. I can't change their habits, so all I can do is figure out how to deal with the situation. I have three alternatives, as far as I can tell. The first is to make a really big effort to be late, but that may be more than I am capable of. The second is to carry reading or writing material with me so that, if I feel like it, I can turn the time to good use. The last is to welcome the opportunity to be present and *not* do anything—just treat this time as a bonus and enjoy it for what it is. The third alternative is the most fruitful, but I suspect that, being me, I will hedge my bets and try the third while having the possibility of the second in my purse.

Lately I have had a recurring dream of being able to fly over whatever is happening. I bounce up with just a small effort and hover above the ground for brief periods. Again, I am not sure I understand the significance of this yet (other than emphasizing that I shouldn't feel so tied down). When I mentioned this dream to an analyst working at the Jung Institute in Switzerland, he smiled and said that perhaps it indicated that there were other ways out of situations than those I had considered, that I could move around and see things from another perspective.

In the spring of 2003 I went on the retreat with Tsoknyi Rinpoche that Jill had told me about. Tsoknyi is a young Dzogchen master, exuberant, clear, concentrated, compassionate, funny, even mischievous, completely accessible, and a wonderful teacher. He reminds me of an English robin—a small bundle of sparkling energy. When I first met him two years earlier, he had described himself in his inimitable English as "a little short Tibetan master with small belly and short neck." When he speaks Tibetan his hands are never still. He uses them constantly to illustrate his stories, even though his audience does not understand a word he is saying until it has been translated. Also he employs whatever is at hand as a prop—the brass bowl, its accompanying stick, his prayer beads, a packet of tissues, the flowers, the water glass. He is a born performer and entertainer, and his mimicking sends people into gales of laughter.

The literal translation of the Tibetan word *Dzogchen* is "Great Perfection," meaning that it is the ultimate teaching, the jewel of the Nyingma school of Tibetan Buddhism. Considered by its adherents to be the most secret teaching of the Buddha, it was brought from India to Tibet in the eighth century by the sages Padmasambhava and Vimilamitra and has been passed down from master to student in the centuries since. It describes the nature of the mind as pure, empty, clear, free, intelligent, and compassionate and offers a way of recognizing and resting in that essence of mind, or *rigpa,* at all times. The "pointing out instructions" for how to achieve this can come only from a teacher and not from a book, tape, or any other form of absent instruction. Not that it can't be described in words, but somehow the words are no longer enlivened when the teacher is not present. Understanding the concept of something is definitely helpful, but it is not the dharma itself. Rinpoche described it as "relative dharma." Words give an indication of what something is, but all words are loaded for us, so we should think of them as just giving a taste of what they describe. What is being pointed out, the experience of rigpa, is something that has been available to us all along but that we tend to miss in every moment. Dzogchen is an utterly simple but very subtle teaching.

I have listened over the years to many Tibetan Buddhist teachers, and although I am very drawn to them as people, I find that they make things SO complicated. By the time they have finished explaining what I call "sacred geography" (the terrain of the mind and how to arrive at and remain in the present moment), any mind you thought you had is completely boggled. I hadn't considered this before the retreat, but now it occurs to me that perhaps this is the aim. And it's not just sacred geography. There's a large element of mathematics involved. There are five of this and three of that, which are then divided into seven thises and four thats. Everything is defined to the nth degree so that there can be no possibility of confusion. Before there is any practical instruction whatsoever, a lama wants to give you an accurate description of everything you might encounter so that you will be able to recognize it when you actually experience it. He doesn't want you to be faced with an unidentified flying object. Tibetans have studied the mind for centuries, and their observations about its nature are scientific and precise. First comes the definition of all the terms, then an explanation of the theory, and finally instructions on what to do. Later, when you actually practice, you will recognize what is happening and know how to deal with it. In some ways it reminds me of how we were taught Latin when I was eleven years old, in that each word and its place in the sentence had to be accurately identified and defined before you were allowed to proceed to the next one.

What Rinpoche presented to us was an entirely new vocabulary. For instance, he described meditation using a method such as focusing on the breath, scanning the body, or repeating a mantra as "*shamatha* with support" and meditation where you keep your mind open to whatever is happening, welcoming it all, and not making any attempt to stick to any one thing as "*shamatha* without support." Shamatha without support is like having a good doorman. The doorman acknowledges whoever enters and leaves the building but doesn't follow anyone into their apartment or down the street. He remains in his place doing his job. In the same way, in shamatha without support the awareness doesn't leave the present moment.

I would have described the first method as "meditation on an object" or "one-pointed meditation" and the other as "meditation without an object." In the first case, there is both a subject (you) and an object, and so there is still duality, but the mind is being trained to be steady and focused (*shamatha* means "calm abiding"). In the second case, there is no particular object and so the whole trap of subject/object is bypassed. The idea is to train in the first until the mind is tranquil and then move effortlessly into the second. Perhaps we should consider them two different phases rather than two methods. What we had come to learn was how to move beyond shamatha without support into rigpa itself.

The terms we use for what we are familiar with become very freighted over time, and there is no way to know whether you are speaking of the same thing as someone else when you use words like "meditation," "God," or "freedom." So adopting a fresh, if alien, vocabulary is liberating because it cuts us loose from so many of our preconceptions and associations. On the other hand, I found myself scurrying to figure out what Rinpoche meant when he used more than one of these unfamiliar terms in the same sentence. It was like translating from another language in order to be able to understand what the speaker was saying rather than being able to think in that language, the way native speakers do. My mind was forced to do a great deal of grappling, but the result was that I had the opportunity to have a completely fresh view of the territory.

Rinpoche told us that the qualities required for this work were faith, perseverance, intelligence, and compassion. Dzogchen is taught only through direct instruction by a teacher, but the difficulty is that it cannot be expressed in words or thought. "This is difficult for me and for you," he said. "I am trying to teach something that cannot be 'talked.' You need to listen in a different way. Do not grasp the words. Relax. Be aware of the teacher, yourself, and the knowledge all held in the same space." He explained that emptiness, clarity, and indivisibility are the attributes of the natural mind—the ground. Generally we see everything in relation to ourselves, but a fish would see things differently. The secret is to step into the present moment, the space between the past and the future, which is the only place where there is freedom and tranquillity.

We have somehow acquired the idea that the workings of our bodies, minds, and emotions need a boss, and we believe that the boss should be "me." According to Buddhism, there is no "me," and everything that goes to make up a human being (or any other creature) functions perfectly well on its own.

Rinpoche described how we fill our minds with ideas about things, concepts of them, and cling to these. It is the clinging that needs to be relinquished not the things themselves. We cling to the notion of an "I," "me," and "mine," and this sets up the duality of subject and object. This happens because the mind doesn't perceive the emptiness of everything. If the mind pursues one thing after another, it will never rest in its true nature.

Each day on retreat I found time to draw a tree or a flower in my sketchbook—unfurling leaves on a delicate maple, the ground cover of star-shaped mauve periwinkles, a few stalks of bamboo. One day it rained, and I stood in the alcove outside the women's room off the main hall and tried to capture a spray of dogwood in a vase. It was an interesting exercise in many respects. The light in the alcove was timed to go on when movement was detected and to go off one minute later. I focused on the creamy bracts, and each time darkness descended I waved my sketchpad wildly at the sensor while keeping my feet firmly planted on the floor so that my perspective would not change.

Each attempt I made to faithfully record what I saw was very frustrating. The blossoms and leaves on their stems seemed to crowd together and obscure my vision. I tried to get down on the paper exactly what was in front of me rather than fudging it, as I so often do when I don't bother to look closely enough to see the shape, the position, and the proportion of each leaf and flower. But somehow the more detail I included, the less it looked like the real thing. I began to see a parallel in the difficulty I was having with accepting Rinpoche's minutely described steps on the path to enlightenment. I liked it when he cut to the chase and told us how to drop into pure awareness, but I grew impatient when he wanted us to study the complex map before we set off.

After a day or so spent defining terms, Rinpoche did give us simple instructions in how to relinquish our hold on our thoughts, liberate them, and rest in the clear emptiness of rigpa. He said that it might not be easy for us to recognize rigpa straightaway, but with continued practice we would become more and more familiar with it. Once we knew how to stop our identification with the conceptual world, we could be at home in the pure emptiness of the real world. This was an invitation to recognize and enjoy that beautiful empty space that is the lucid and formless nature of the mind rather than continue to behave the way we have always done, allowing the mind to chat to itself all the time. The mind is such a gossip. The trick is to be like the night sky. Instead of focusing on any single star, be aware of the wide-open glory of the heavens in which each star rests.

When you go on retreat, reentry into daily life can be hard, particularly if you have done very intense practice. It feels as though nature is making a concerted effort to redress the balance and restore you to your normal unconscious state. Returning home on similar occasions, I have often felt that I had taken one step forward only to take two steps back. This time, however, I felt as if I had been forced to take three steps back.

First, I came home with the heaviest cold I have had in years, garnered from two meditators snuffling away beside me for a week. For five days I sneezed constantly and violently, except when I was either eating or sleeping. Then I went out and bought a bottle of Irish whiskey at nine in the morning and started dosing myself with lemon, honey, hot water, and plenty of the strong stuff. For a long time now my preferred form of medicine has been whiskey. I have enormous faith in its restorative powers and banishing ability. On this occasion it took just one day to do the trick. The next morning I awoke completely cured. It is true that perhaps the cold had run its natural course, but we all like to believe in the occasional miracle.

Then, on my first full day back in New York I spent three hours in the waiting room of a mammography unit and finally walked out in a huff. I had spent two hours there several weeks earlier and had been recalled for a better shot of my right breast. On the first occasion I had sat there patiently for two hours and was then told that I was fine after all—which may or may not have been true. This time I waited two hours for the mammogram and another hour for the doctor to read it, which she had not done by the time I left. Why do clinics schedule so many patients at the same time if they can't cope with them?

During the retreat there had been yoga classes every evening so that we could get our bodies back into shape for the following day's sitting torture. I was too exhausted to attend on the first few days and participated in only one class, during which we draped our spines over cushions and allowed ourselves to sink back into them. Somehow this resulted in all my knobbles rearranging themselves in a higgledy-piggledy fashion, which is not the way they are supposed to be. I went to visit the chiropractor on my return, and he decompressed me somewhat, but a few vertebrae still stuck in and out in ways they had never done before. I prayed that they would gradually find their way home on their own.

There is one more thing I haven't mentioned. When I reflected on my experience at the retreat, I came to the stark realization that I have been meditating for over forty years without really enjoying it. For me it is something to be endured rather than enjoyed. Now what do I do? One friend asked me whether that meant I would stop meditating. I said, "Probably not." There are many things I do in my life that I don't enjoy much, but that doesn't necessarily mean that I stop doing them. I am always hoping that eventually I will start to enjoy them, at least occasionally. Anyway, isn't the point of spiritual work to get beyond the like/don't like hurdle? But it is sad because I know many people who look forward to sitting on their cushions; I turn out not to be one of them.

Ram Dass came to one of the readings of my first book that I gave in the Bay Area. One of the passages I chose to read was about the importance of the space between one thing and another. Afterward he grinned and said to me, "Watch this space," the familiar slogan on so many billboards, and I responded with "Mind the gap," the announcement made on the London underground trains each time the doors open and people step out onto the platform. However you choose to describe it, it is what is not there that is important.

Entering the Magic Kingdom

> Then comes the moment
> of feeling the wings that you've grown,
> lifting.

"Unfold Your Own Myth," Rumi, *translated by Coleman Barks*

 In 2003, I took a trip to Brazil, which came about in a very strange way. Thirty years earlier I had published a remarkable book by Frederick Franck, *The Zen of Seeing*, about drawing exactly what you see. Frederick points out that although you have lived with lettuces all your life, until you have tried to draw one, you have never noticed "what makes a lettuce a lettuce rather than a curly kale." The book was tremendously successful and has now sold over a quarter of a million copies. I never got around to following its instructions until Wanxin suggested I keep a sketchbook. Now, at last, I understand that

you have to keep drawing something over and over again to refine your vision.

I edited three other books by Frederick, but over the years I have seen less and less of him, partly because he lives several hours' drive upstate in Warwick, New York. In December 2002, his wife, Claske, called to ask if I would go and visit them because Frederick had a project on which he needed my professional advice. He is now in his midnineties and I realized that it might be the very last time I saw him. I agreed to go, and he offered to have a friend drive me up and back.

So one fine morning a dark blue car drew up outside my building and I climbed in. It was driven by a Latvian herpetologist (a specialist in reptiles) in his midseventies named Janis Rozé, a professor emeritus of biology at City College in New York and one of the most engaging men I have ever met. His mind spins at a mile a minute, and he is brimming with energy and goodwill. During the course of the day I learned that his wife, Amanda, comes from Colombia, is considerably younger than he is, and is also a biologist. They have two boys of their own and recently adopted a three-year-old autistic boy who is the child of one of her cousins. Now that Santiago is in a big, loving family, he has started to speak and enjoy life.

Janis and I started talking as we drove north, and we never stopped. We took care of what we had to do at Frederick's and then drove back. Halfway home, by which time Janis had decided that he and I had probably met in a previous life, he asked me if I would like to join him and his family in Brazil where they go every summer. I was more than taken aback. He described this little place called Búzios on the Atlantic coast three hours north of Rio de Janeiro, made famous by Brigitte Bardot in the early 1970s. Janis told me that they go there every year with a group of friends from Argentina. At this time of year, off-season and with the temperature in the seventies, the rates are even cheaper than usual (everything in Brazil is cheap for Americans) and since the manager is an old friend, Janis could get me a 50 percent discount. The whole thing sounded so enchanting that I was tempted, but I suggested that I meet his wife and children first. I pointed out that they might not like me (and, of course, I might not like them, although I didn't mention this), and that he shouldn't invite me until his family had decided that they too wanted me to join them. So I went to dinner at his house one night a few weeks later, and we all got along fine. In the ensuing months he often e-mailed me early in the morning, and one day even came to my apartment for coffee, bringing white peonies (which I painted) and berries to eat.

I had asked when the trip would take place and he said he would let me know, but as the months passed there was no word of a precise date, and I began to wonder whether he really meant what he said. Then, at the beginning of July, he announced that he and his family would be leaving on August 10. He had been waiting to hear from his friends in Buenos Aires about the date they would arrive in Búzios. Apparently, South Americans don't plan as far ahead as North Americans do. So suddenly I had to make a decision. I had never been to South America and was unwilling to pass up the opportunity, but I was a little concerned about the cost of getting there.

It turned out to be $1,100 round trip and twelve hours' flying time. Then I discovered that I could use my seventy-one thousand frequent flyer miles, accumulated from all my trips to England to see my mother over the last eleven years. So I bought a ticket for the price of the airport taxes: $51 and a few cents. Not being an American citizen, I didn't need a visa, but I did need a passport valid for six months beyond the date of arrival. Unfortunately, I was two weeks short of the required six months. So I moved heaven and earth to try to get a new passport in time.

You can no longer get passports at the British consulate in New York but have to apply to the embassy in Washington, which warns that in the summer it can take up to four weeks. I was very nervous that the new passport wouldn't arrive in time, but in the end it did.

There is another story connected with my trip. In 1987 I received a copy of a sumptuously handbound book called *The Battle of Kurukshetra* by a writer in India by the name of Maggi Lidchi-Grassi, who had sent it at the suggestion of Doris Lessing, who was a mutual friend. I knew Doris from when she was published by Knopf. By that time Doris had been encouraging Maggi's writing for twenty years.

Maggi was born in Paris, of Spanish Jewish parents, married an Italian, was personal secretary to the Mother at the Sri Aurobindo Ashram in Pondicherry in Southern India for several years, adopted five children, founded a complementary healing center in Auroville, plays the lyre, and has remained at the ashram for thirty-three years. She has had several books published in England, France, Spain, and the United States and many more in India.

The Battle of Kurukshetra is the first of three wondrous volumes that retell the great Indian epic the *Mahabharata*, about the trials and tribulations of Prince

Arjuna and his brothers. I loved that first volume—all about surrender—but felt that it would not appeal to a large audience in the United States, so I did not suggest that Maggi send it to any publishers. Two years later the second volume appeared in India, and she sent me a copy of that too. After reading each book I wrote to thank her and tell her how much I enjoyed her writing. Finally, last year, I received the third volume, *The Great Golden Sacrifice of the Mahabharata*, and our correspondence started up again. This time Maggi enlisted my help in finding an American publisher. I did my best but was not successful. However, what burgeoned was our correspondence. Maggi wrote me long letters in spidery black handwriting, signing them with a drawing of her long-haired, smiling, seraphic self, hands joined in namaste.

From time to time she would describe snippets of her life and her friendship with Doris, and she would send copies of her other books. The letters and packages were often misaddressed, but they eventually made their way to me and always contained dried pink and purple bougainvillea bracts (they look like petals, but technically they aren't), the color of the first book she had sent me. These I started to gather in a Tibetan brass prayer bowl I keep on my coffee table. Maggi told me that the Mother had called these flowers "protection flowers." Occasionally, I would send her books I had edited that I thought she would enjoy.

After I had amassed a goodly sheaf of her letters (and bougainvillea), a registered envelope arrived from India. Inside was a tiny packet of white powder, which was, according to Maggi, "the most precious thing I have in the house—a dynamization of something the Mother gave me and which has her subtle physical energy." Maggi didn't mention what the substance was, other than that it was a homeopathic remedy, but she recommended that I take it either during or after meditation. Neither did she say what it was for, but she implied that other people who had taken it had had profound and moving experiences.

I kept it on my desk for a few weeks, waiting for the right moment, and then, one quiet afternoon a couple of days before leaving for Brazil, I ingested the treasure she had bequeathed me. I sat down to meditate, and after a little while put the powder under my tongue and continued to meditate. I didn't taste anything special, and after about twenty minutes, not knowing how long it might take to work, I got up off my cushion. I was moved to go the Auroville website (which I had not done before) and look at a picture of the Mother and read a little of her teachings. Then I settled down and listened to some plaintive reed flute music that I had bought in Turkey at the tomb of Rumi, where it is played constantly, and I began to read. Still nothing happened, and so I resumed my evening routine. I'm not sure what I expected. Perhaps the kind of experience others report when they take mind-expanding drugs? (I've never taken drugs.) Certainly an opening of consciousness. But everything proceeded as usual, and I felt somewhat let down.

That night I had a dream. I don't often remember my dreams, but I managed to retrieve some of this one. I was away from home and in the company of people I had known many years earlier. We were about to fly home from wherever we were, and I went to put some papers in my suitcase and discovered that all my possessions, money, and airline ticket, even the suitcase itself, had vanished without a trace. Then, as I often do when I am in a dream and caught in circumstances I don't know how to deal with, I forced myself to wake up.

I can't tell whether the dream was related to the Mother's thirty-year-old potion, but it certainly highlighted my attachment to all the ways I have tried to shape my life to make it "just right" for emancipation of some kind. Perhaps the dream was telling me to surrender all my ties to the past, everything I have done to "earn" self-realization. That all I need is to be present, just as I am, and with no baggage. Could this be the Mother's gift to me? It's not that I haven't always known this in my heart, but understanding something intellectually and putting it into practice are two different kettles of fish.

The following day I described to Janis what had (not) happened when I took the powder, and my subsequent dream. He said that it was wonderful that we were about to depart for Búzios, which was such a magical place in itself that no one ever knew what was going to happen. He and his friends always go there with no preconceived ideas. So I felt poised for something but did not know what that something might be.

In middle age I began to succumb to panic attacks. They generally occur a few days before I am about to set off on a journey. I wake in the wee hours of the morning, troubled at the thought of the many things I need to do before I leave, my stomach tightens and then swings violently, and I can quickly and easily be reduced to the dry heaves. This will happen morning after morning, even though I take care of each of the tasks I am afraid I will forget or not have time for. None of them remains undone by the day of my departure.

Not until I am checked in at the airport or en-

sconced in my seat on the bus or train am I able to relax. For some reason I am constantly fearful that I
will, through some unforeseen (but vividly imagined)
disaster, fail to arrive in time for the plane or whatever it is. My brother Chris once asked me if I had, in
fact, ever missed a flight, and it goes without saying
that I had not. He pointed out that my anxiety was,
therefore, unreasonable.

"Of course," I cried. "This is not about reason. I
am an extremely reasonable person, and this surge of
unreasonableness is very distressing."

But he persisted: "It's not as if there won't be another plane. Even if you missed the one you had
planned to take, you could always get the next one."

This anxiety about traveling has crept up on me. I
don't know where it came from nor why it lingers.
You'd think my psyche would have calmed down after all my positive experiences, but it hasn't.

How often we focus on the idea of something rather
than the experience itself, without realizing that the
idea is usually a great deal more daunting than the real
thing! What happens to me before I set off on a trip is
an extreme example of an insubstantial notion using
my strength and energy to bolster itself. But there are
numerous smaller instances that occur throughout
the day, and they are so insidious I hardly notice them.

I am reminded of an incident that took place many years ago. My parents and I took my son Adam to the movies for the first time on Christmas Day when he was almost two. Adam and I didn't have a television in those days, although he had undoubtedly been exposed to it outside our home. He had a passion for dragons when he was small, so we took him to see a Walt Disney movie that featured a dragon. He sat on my knee transfixed throughout the film, and when it was over and the lights came back on, he dashed to the front of the theater crying, "Dwagon, dwagon," and tried to climb up onto the stage. It was hard to explain that the dragon wasn't real and therefore not lurking behind the blank screen.

All this was the background to my trip.

The afternoon of my departure arrived, and the first thing that went wrong was that the car I had ordered to take me to the airport did not turn up and I had to commandeer a taxi. Then the plane was an hour late arriving at La Guardia and, consequently, an hour late leaving. There was only an hour-and-a-half window between our arrival in Miami and our flight to Rio de Janeiro, and by the time we reached Miami at 11:30 at night, all the connecting flights for South America had already left. We were told that we would have to wait until the same flight the following night in order to proceed with our journey and that we would be housed and fed at an airport hotel in the meantime. Our luggage would be held for us and put on the plane the next day, which meant that we had no extra clothes or toiletries. This was the kind of scenario I had been afraid of from the very beginning. (It turned out that two different friends had also had premonitions that something would go wrong but hadn't liked to mention it.) Janis and his family were flying via Washington, D.C., and were due to arrive in Rio three hours after me and we had arranged where we would meet the driver who was picking us up. Neither of us had a cell phone, and from the start I kept worrying what we would do if either of us missed a connection, but each time I started fretting about this, I remembered what Janis had said about magic and told myself that nothing untoward would happen.

Well after midnight, when we had checked into the hotel, a young Brazilian woman was kind enough to call Búzios and tell them in Portuguese what had happened, asking that Janis be advised on his arrival and that another car be sent to the airport to pick me up the following day. I speak no Portuguese, and my Spanish is limited to what I learned in three months of business Spanish (which I have never had any occasion to use) when I was eighteen plus what I overhear in the subway in New York City. This means that I can usually figure out what people are talking about but not what they are actually saying. The next morning I examined my new boarding pass and saw that it was for São Paolo and not Rio. Another blow. I called American Airlines and was told that the direct flight was full; I would need to change planes in São Paolo and would now arrive two hours later than I had anticipated. Which required another call to Búzios.

It was freezing cold in the hotel and intensely hot in the summer sun outside. The only redeeming feature of those long hours in Miami was the company of some of the other passengers who had interesting tales to tell. From a gemology journalist (who had traveled from Philadelphia and also missed his connection) I learned that there had been a young Brazilian couple on his flight who went berserk when they discovered that they couldn't continue immediately to Rio. They were getting married the next day, had invited four hundred guests to celebrate with them, and were carrying the wedding gown on the plane. My plight paled in comparison to theirs. I felt queasy, lethargic, and helpless, but at least I wasn't going to miss my wedding. The place I found myself in seemed more like Miasma than Miami, but it was no good bewailing the fact that without our suitcases we had very little to occupy our time and couldn't even take a swim in the hotel pool. (I made a mental note to pack my swimsuit in my carry-on luggage on all future trips.) Things were as they were. Still, it wasn't easy to relinquish the feeling of endurance that kept surfacing, and to remember that each moment is here to be lived, even if it takes place in an airport hotel.

Late in the evening I boarded the plane to São Paolo, where the airport was calm and spacious and masseuses offered backrubs at every turn (I almost succumbed). I connected with the plane to Rio without further mishap, but I was still nervous about whether my luggage was on board, whether anyone would be waiting for me at the barrier when I arrived, and if there wasn't, how I would manage. As it turned out, the Brazilian student sitting next to me on the half-hour flight from São Paolo gave me her address and phone number in Rio and invited me to call on her if I needed to, and she waited until I found my driver and was in good hands, bless her.

Several hours later I arrived safely in Búzios and met up with Janis. "Here I am," I said, "only twenty-four hours late."

"It takes some people longer than others," he responded, and I suspected that he wasn't talking about the length of the journey but about the fact that I had at last missed a plane. It had taken me my whole life to be so magnificently late. Perhaps this was an auspicious beginning after all.

I was soon ensconced in an airy, whitewashed room with a tiny balcony overlooking a garden with mauve bougainvillea trees. The hotel was situated on a spectacular headland, nestled in five hundred acres of scrubby Mata Atlantica forest, which is a combination of deciduous trees, epiphytes, lichen, Spanish moss, creepers, and cactus. I was told that snakes and a troop of monkeys inhabited the forest, but we never caught sight of either. The place is a good fifteen minutes' drive from the town of Búzios itself, so we were quite a distance from any shops, boats, and the more than thirty exquisite beaches on the peninsula.

Early in the morning I often sat on my balcony and watched the sun spill its light across the landscape, illuminating each white house with its terra cotta roof and chimney, the forest behind all the buildings, and in the distance the silhouette of the blue-gray mountains. The still almost-full moon gradually bleached away as the sun's rays grew in strength. Mourning doves sped by in pairs, occasionally an emerald hummingbird hovered in the branches, tiny brown warblers sang, and a raucous flock of small green parrots, which I never managed to see close up, called to one another from all sides. And ever in the background I could hear the roll and crash of the waves in the cove below.

The twenty people who traveled each summer to be with Janis came mainly from Buenos Aires. The group, which called itself "Be Human," didn't seem to follow any particular spiritual practice. It met only in Búzios and not throughout the year, although some members were also involved in traditions such as Tibetan Buddhism. One man told me that he was taking a course to learn how to clean his chakras, and it goes without saying that no one would want to have dirty chakras.

There seemed to be little advance planning each day, which was hard for me to get my mind around, and whatever plans there were were made in Spanish. Halfway through the week we did receive a schedule, but as it turned out almost nothing listed actually took place as planned. I discovered that in South America, things tend not to happen where and when you expect them to, so you might as well not plan too far ahead. Something will happen somewhen and somewhere, but no one really knows what, when, and where it will be (yet). When whatever it is occurs, you simply welcome it. In the past I have always expected the worst and tried for the best, which is a rather antagonistic way of facing the world.

I often harbor a foolish desire to know what is going to happen before I embark on something. On this trip, my desires were spectacularly unfulfilled and all the turmoil I experienced was a vivid lesson in the uncertainty principle. As Pico Iyer remarked on my return, this was an "adventure into surprise and serendipity and all the ways our assumptions are overturned in just the way we don't expect them to be."

I firmly believe that self-help books sell so well in this country because Americans are addicted to fantasy. As many of my friends know, I include weather forecasts in this category (fantasy, not self-help) and maintain that only in the United States could there be a weather channel on television. Day after day and hour after hour, we are treated to precise descriptions of what to expect. Yet, although the meteorologists are always right about the weather itself, they tend to be wrong about both the time and the place. Fantasy is so irresistible because everyone is under the spell of what might be possible if only the present circumstances didn't apply.

The more I observed Janis, the more I realized how like Frederick he had become. I knew that they had been friends for years and that now that Frederick was nearing the end of his life, Janis drove up to see him almost every week, doing what he could to be of support and good cheer. Janis has the same shaped white beard, the same jaw that juts out when he speaks, the same urgency about saving humanity from itself before it is too late. An intrepid, visionary man with a great big heart, not knowing what words and actions will come through him until they are presented, and then offering whatever arrives to those around him. A prophet, yes, but without fire and brimstone. Here was a man inviting us to surrender our individuality, begin to know who we really are, and acknowledge that our work is to conduct the energy of the universe.

On most days we had some kind of movement activity, and we also met in the candlelit *oratorio escondido,* a tiny hexagonal chapel hidden away in the woods, to listen to Janis and offer our own observations. During one poignant gathering, he gently urged us to remember our function as human beings and live our lives as instruments of the Divine, not wasting any opportunity through attachment to our own individual goals. "Open the gate with love," he said again and again. I took this to refer to the entrance to our hearts, which we guard so carefully, but perhaps he also meant that our role was to provide access for others, to be the means by which they too realize what they are in these bodies for. In Turkey I had discovered that the Persian word *dervish* means "threshold," and for me this image of someone standing at the doorway between earth and heaven is reminiscent of the Sanskrit *tirtha*, meaning "crossing over, ford, the confluence of two rivers," and also the word used to describe a great Hindu saint.

During these sessions I noticed my reluctance to remain in the present. My mind was always wandering off, doing its best to be anywhere but here. Grasping at the words of Amanda's translation (she always sat between the two of us who didn't speak Spanish and kindly translated), I would lose the sound of the cicadas, the crashing of the waves, and the breeze cooling the back of my neck. We cling to a small part of what is going on and miss the whole. We want more or something that isn't being offered right now, and we suspect that whatever we receive may not meet our expectations. We hope for too much, believing that it is our due, that that is what others experience. We concentrate on our hopes and fears. "Now is the winter of our discontent," said Shakespeare's Richard III. Yet the bleakness we feel is because we weren't "now" before we received something, and once the event turns out to be different from our expectations, we are still not in the present moment. More often than not we don't get what we dreamed of, and then we focus on our "misfortune" rather than what we had all along—focusing on the negative and not the positive, in a very real way. I don't like it when book reviewers do that, but I've not been willing to admit that this is the lens through which I view life almost all of the time.

One day it rained for hours, and I sat reading *By the Lake*, John McGahern's novel about country life in Ireland. There I stumbled over this sentence: "They all want it and they're all afraid." The woman who makes this sage pronouncement is describing men's desire for sex, but her observation is applicable to anyone in any situation. We are so often afraid of what might or might not happen.

On another morning I stayed in my room and painted a hibiscus. When I had finished, I left the painting to dry on the ledge in front of the window where I had been working. I wandered around the garden, drawing another hibiscus and also a crown of thorns. When I returned, the maid was sweeping the room and her cleaning materials were sitting right on top of my painting. So much for art appreciation.

I was promised that there would be magic in Búzios, but if it was there, it didn't appear in any form I recognized at the time. However, Janis and his family stayed longer than I did, and a small miracle happened in their presence. For some years, Amanda and her American colleague, John, had been doing research on the dark red hardwood Brazil tree, after which the country is named, and the day after I left for New York, the whole group made an expedition on foot to where it grows in the forest. On the path they caught a brief glimpse of an iridescent blue-and-turquoise morpho butterfly, whose wingspan is more than four inches. Amanda, John, and Janis made a final visit to the tree after everyone else had returned to Argentina. The two men were standing a little way off when a beautiful "blue" began fluttering around Amanda, who was making some scientific measurements of the tree. Then it flew over to where the men were before returning to dance in the air around Amanda once more. Soon it was joined by another great "blue" and then two more, all whirling around her. One butterfly alighted briefly on her foot and another on her shoulder. They continued their ephemeral dance for about ten minutes before vanishing once more into the forest.

I suspect that what hindered me from witnessing any magic was my expectation of it. If you look for something special, it usually doesn't manifest, but if you keep your eye on the ordinary, something extraordinary may indeed appear. You create the opportunity for magic only by giving up your preconceptions.

In Búzios, several of us took a walk each day before breakfast. We always took the same route, stopping for coffee at a place on the main road before retracing our steps. In the beginning everything looked the same, but soon I began to see a new plant here, a burst seedpod there, a yellow-breasted bird on the telegraph wire. There was always something fresh to observe. We tell ourselves that we have "been there, done that," and we yearn to move on. This is one of the things that inexorably takes us away from wherever we happen to be: the notion that there is nothing interesting where we are. *Interesting* means *being in between*, which would indicate a lack of attachment, yet that is not how we think of it. If we are in between, then we are in the open space that connects one thing to another, that joins everyone.

I returned from South America with two things: a splendid black shoulder bag made out of a single extremely long zipper, which I bought on Tartaruga Beach the day we went out in a boat, and the hard-won understanding that the best approach to life is to float, to rest on the surface of wherever I find myself, not grasping at anything and not expecting that I will either sink or soar.

When I was en route for Brazil and during my time there, the notion of accepting whatever comes along and not expecting things to go according to plan seemed very alien. I felt thwarted at every turn. But now that I am home, reflecting on what happened and also how this book took shape, I am amazed. I see that ever since I quit my job, I have been moving in the opposite direction from my natural tendencies. It hasn't been easy, but I have tried to relax my grip on the world and allow things to happen more organically. Of course, everything happens organically anyway, whether we want it to or not, but nowadays I try to go with the grain rather than against it.

I recognize that in many ways this book is an example of floating, although I carefully concealed this from myself throughout the process. I didn't know what I would be writing about when I began; I wrote only when something happened in my life or in my mind; instead of worrying about the theme of each chapter I acknowledged that my latest minirevelations, once they had accumulated on the page, were different aspects of the same truth and therefore belonged together; and the chapter titles always arrived unannounced and in their own sweet time.

Alleluia!

A Note on the Art

The illustrations are paintings I did between 2000 and 2003.

Chinese and Japanese brushes come in many different shapes and sizes. I use brown sable or weasel hard-hair brushes for stalks and small details because they have strength and resilience. For leaves and blossoms, which need full soft strokes, I use white sheep- or rabbit-hair brushes that hold more water. Both kinds of brushes have light bamboo handles. I use Chinese liquid black ink made from the soot of burnt pinewood and tubes of Chinese watercolors.

Although in the West the paper is called "rice paper," it is not made from rice but from various plant materials such as mulberry, sandalwood, or bamboo. I use single or double Shuen paper manufactured in China. This is flimsy, unsized, and as porous as blotting paper.

About the Author

Toinette Lippe was born in London, where she began her publishing career at André Deutsch. In 1964 she came to New York City "for a year," worked at Simon and Schuster for three years, and then at Alfred A. Knopf as reprint rights director and editor for thirty-two years. In 1989, while still at Knopf, she founded Bell Tower, an imprint devoted to books that nourish the soul, illuminate the mind, and speak directly to the heart. Since 2000 she has continued as editorial director of Bell Tower, in addition to doing freelance editing and writing. Her first book, *Nothing Left Over: A Plain and Simple Life*, was published in 2002. She lives on the Upper West Side of Manhattan.